FLORIDA CITRUS COOKBOOK

Marmac Publishing Company, Inc.

Distributed U.S.A. by Pelican Publishing Company, Inc.

**Recipes and contents of this cookbook have been approved by
the Florida Department of Citrus.**

*Recipe development and photograph food styling: D-A-Y Kitchens, Dudley-Anderson-Yutzy,
The Ogilvy and Mather Public Relations Company, New York, N.Y.*

Designer: Paul Kirouac, A Good Thing, Inc., New York, N.Y.

*Photography: Gus Francisco Photography, New York, N.Y. Pages 6-7, 10-11, 28-9, 43, 60-1,
108-9, 134-5, 180-1, Front and Back Covers.
Walter Storck Studio, Inc., New York, N.Y. Pages 17, 23, 33, 39, 49, 55, 67,
73, 79, 85, 91, 99, 119, 127, 133, 141, 147, 151, 157, 173.
Bill Helms, Inc., New York, N.Y. Page 163.
Vincent Lee, New York, N.Y. Page 167.*

Publisher and Executive Editor: Marge McDonald
Editor: Elizabeth Speir
Contributing Editor: William Schemmel

Published by: Marmac Publishing Company, Atlanta, GA.
*Distributed in USA by: Pelican Publishing Company, 1101 Monroe
Street, Gretna, LA. 70053*

ISBN: 0-939944-44-8

Library of Congress Number: 85-072517

Manufactured in the United States of America

Contents

Front Cover photograph: Scalloped Fruit Cup, page 145
Back Cover photograph: Grapefruit with Berries and Cream, page 144

Foreword

Florida, with its warm climate and tropical rainfall, is America's number one producer of all citrus varieties. Here oranges, grapefruit, tangerines and tangelos grow sweet and juicy, and thin-skinned.

The vitality of the Florida citrus industry is a tribute in part to the Florida Citrus Commission, organized at the request of the industry itself by legislative acts beginning in 1935. Under the direction of the Commission, the Florida Department of Citrus administers the Florida Citrus Code which regulates the packing, processing, labeling and handling of citrus fruits and juices from Florida to assure you, the consumer, of quality citrus products.

In its efforts to continually provide consumers with meaningful measures of quality assurance, the industry introduced "Florida's Seal of Approval" to identify orange juice packed to the state's strict standards, which exceed those of the federal government. Consumers are guaranteed that brands displaying "Florida's Seal of Approval" contain only 100% pure juice without sweeteners, preservatives or additives.

Celebrating its Golden Anniversary in 1985, 50 years of dedication to quality and consumer satisfaction, the Florida Citrus Commission is proud to endorse this wonderful collection of tasty Florida citrus recipes.

Enjoy!

Florida Citrus Commission

Chairman

Introduction

Introduction

Citrus is the perfect food partner for the lifestyles of the '80s. Available in fruit or juice form the year 'round, so cool, so casual, so complementary of today's dining, it might have been discovered only yesterday. In truth, citrus has been a welcome companion of gracious living throughout the ages. It is one of mankind's oldest, truest and most delicious fruits.

But where did citrus come from?

No one can say for certain, but perhaps instead of an apple, Eve was actually tempted by the luscious beauty of an orange. After all, in Greek mythology, oranges were known as "golden apples." Mighty Jupiter presented an orange to his beloved Juno as a wedding gift and to this day, the exquisite scent of orange blossoms remains a symbol of love eternal.

Since the days of Greek legend, food for the gods has become sustenance of mortal man. Malaysians enjoyed citrus thousands of years ago. Later, 27 different citrus varieties flourished in China at the court of the Great Kubla Khan. The fruit served as a gift for emperors, as a source of pleasant fragrance for court ladies, as a theme for poetry and painting and as a symbol of happiness.

In Chinese junks and in merchant ships, the fruit journeyed as seeds and trees to Japan and the South Pacific, and much later to Arabia and Africa with Arab sailors. In Africa, the fruit was discovered by Greek and Roman soldiers who took it back to the Mediterranean, where it thrived at the time of Christ.

During the 6th and 7th centuries, Muslim armies brought war and oranges from India to Spain, leaving a path of orange groves that flourished particularly well in Spain. The Renaissance artists especially loved oranges and, because it was commonly believed that they originated in Palestine, orange trees dotted the landscapes of holy paintings. The great artists painted Virgins with oranges, saints with oranges—and Italian royalty with oranges.

The excitement over the exotic fruit caught the attention of royalty to the north. At the close of the 15th century, Charles VIII of France set off to Italy and fell in love with Italian art, architecture and oranges. He returned home with an entourage of Italian gardeners. At Charles' chateau in Amboise, the gardeners built the first orangerie, an elaborate indoor grove devoted to the cultivation of oranges.

For the next two centuries, no French reign was successful until the king built an indoor grove more elaborate than that of his predecessor. At the palace of Versailles, the great innovator King Louis XIV dreamed up a C-shaped indoor grove, 1200 feet in circumference. It served as a romantic setting for masked balls and garden parties.

Louis' gardeners learned how to parch the trees to the point of death and then revive them to bloom almost on demand, providing the Sun King with fruit throughout the year. Trees in the orangeries were planted in giant boxes and moved indoors and out with the seasons. The floors were built with holes, under which great pans of water steamed, the better to convince the oranges that they were in the tropics.

The craze for oranges spread still further north. By Elizabethan times, oranges were common enough to be sold in English theaters for sixpence. In Queen Victoria's day, oranges were a treasured Christmas gift in England.

Citrus arrived in the United States when Christopher Columbus and succeeding Spanish conquistadores brought the first oranges to Florida. The subtropical climate and citrus were made for each other. By the end of the American Revolution, Florida oranges were so plentiful that they were exported back to Europe for sale there.

Grapefruit was a later arrival to our shores. Like oranges, this tart-sweet fruit traces its ancestry to Malaysia, where it was known as the pomelo or pummelo. Grapefruit was carried on trade routes across India, China, Persia and to the shores of the Mediterranean. From there, seeds were brought across the Atlantic to the West Indies. A Frenchman, Count Odette Phillipe, planted the first grapefruit trees in Florida around Tampa Bay in 1823. Today, Florida produces more grapefruit than the rest of the world combined.

The tangerine, cousin of the Chinese mandarin orange, is named for Tangiers, the North African port from which this citrus was originally shipped to Florida. In the United States, a zipper-like peel and easily-separating sections have long made tangerines a favorite for out-of-hand eating. Tangerines have been cross-pollinated with oranges to create the temple orange, and with grapefruit to produce another citrus variety, the popular tangelo.

Citrus adds a refreshing zest to soups, salads and breads, and gives a sophisticated flair to vegetables and relishes. It coaxes hidden flavors from robust meats and sauces, artfully complements fowl and delicate seafood, and makes elegant desserts, bracing coolers and cocktails. To top it all, garnishes sculpted from citrus raise ordinary dishes to the sublime.

Citrus, the modern-day choice for excellent eating, enjoys worldwide popularity. Jupiter and his fellow dieties would surely be astonished at how far we mortals have taken their "golden apples."

Beverages

Beverages

Oh, the versatility of Florida citrus juices! Sensational alone, they are a knock-out when blended into cooling apertifs, cocktails, hot drinks and fruit smoothies. With their clean, sparkling taste, their powerpack of nutrition, citrus juices start you off on the right foot in the morning and buoy you straight through the day.

Beverages made with citrus juices not only taste good, they look great, too! Whether orange, yellow, pink, or mixed and garnished with other ingredients for a variety of pretty colors, citrus drinks can have a pleasing effect on the eye, making them an important element of meals and snacks.

Citrus juices give the traditional cocktail party a contemporary verve. Traditionally coupled with popular wines and liquors, citrus juices also offer the new breed of light drinkers a tart and healthy beverage alternative.

Perhaps the greatest talent of vivacious citrus juices is an ability to harmonize with luscious fruits, spices, cordials, even vegetables. The result is a bevy of beverage recipes for every occasion, every season.

Opening photograph; 1-r: Tropical Breeze, page 13; Mimosa Cocktail, page 13; Orange Fantasia, page 14; Grapefruit Spritzer, page 14; Frosted Orange Creme, page 15

Elegant in stemmed coupe glasses.

TROPICAL BREEZE

1	cup Florida grapefruit juice
¾	cup light rum
1	large banana, peeled, cut in chunks
3	tablespoons canned cream of coconut
2	cups ice cubes
	Orange slices and maraschino cherries (optional)

Combine all ingredients in a blender. Cover. Process until mixture is slushy. Add ½ to 1 cup more ice, if necessary.

Garnish with an orange slice and maraschino cherry, if desired.

Serve immediately.

YIELD: 3 servings.

Photograph, page 10, left.

MIMOSA COCKTAIL

| 1 | bottle (750 ML.) champagne, chilled |
| 3 | cups Florida orange juice, chilled |

In champagne glasses, combine equal parts of champagne and orange juice.

Serve immediately.

YIELD: 12 servings.

Photograph, page 10, center left.

ORANGE FANTASIA

1½ cups Florida orange juice
1 cup (½ pint) orange sherbet
1 Florida orange slice, halved
2 sprigs fresh mint leaves

Pour orange juice into blender container; add orange sherbet. Cover and process at medium speed until smooth. Or, sherbet may be softened slightly, added to orange juice and beaten with a rotary beater until smooth. If desired, pour over cracked ice.

Garnish with an orange slice and fresh mint leaves.

YIELD: 2½ cups or 2 servings.

Photograph, page 11, center.

Add vodka, if desired.

GRAPEFRUIT SPRITZERS

1 can (6 ounces) Florida frozen concentrated
grapefruit juice, thawed, undiluted
2¼ cups chilled club soda or seltzer
Fresh strawberries

Pour undiluted grapefruit juice concentrate into pitcher. Slowly pour in club soda; mix well. Serve in punch cups.

Garnish with fresh strawberries.

YIELD: 4 servings.

Photograph, page 11, lower right.

FROSTED ORANGE CREME

1   *cup (½ pint) vanilla ice cream*
1   *cup club soda*
4   *tablespoons Florida frozen concentrated orange*
          juice, thawed, undiluted
          Heavy cream, whipped
          Grated orange peel

Combine all ingredients in blender container. Cover. Process at high speed about 30 seconds. Serve in large goblets.

Garnish with whipped cream and sprinkle with grated orange peel.

YIELD: 2 servings.

Photograph, page 11, far right.

THE TALLAHASSEE TALL ONE

1½   *cups Florida grapefruit juice*
½   *cup cream-flavored soda*
          Drop grenadine syrup
          Crushed ice
          Mint sprigs
          Grapefruit peel

Mix together grapefruit juice, cream soda and syrup until syrup is evenly distributed. Pour over crushed ice in tall, thin glass.

Garnish with mint. Attach long strip of grapefruit peel to straw when served or add grapefruit wedge.

YIELD: 1 tall serving.

Photograph, page 17, top.

The zippy, refreshing flavor is an instant pick-me-up.

THE T.G.I. FLORIDA

2	cups Florida grapefruit juice
1½	cups Florida tangerine juice
1	cup apricot nectar
1	cup seltzer or club soda
	Crushed ice
	Slices of pink grapefruit, halved

Mix together grapefruit and tangerine juices, apricot nectar and seltzer; pour over crushed ice in tall pitcher.

Garnish with slices of pink grapefruit.

YIELD: 4 servings.

Photograph, opposite page.

"Steep thyself in a bowl of summertime." —Virgil

EVERGLADE PUNCH

2	cups water
1	cup sugar
1	cup packed, fresh mint leaves
1	quart Florida grapefruit juice
1	cup seltzer or club soda
	Molded ice ring or ice cubes
	Florida grapefruit slices, halved
	Fresh mint

In small saucepan, combine water and sugar; boil 5 minutes; add mint leaves and boil 5 to 10 minutes longer, or until mixture becomes light green and has reduced to 1½ cups liquid. Remove from heat; cool to room temperature. Strain syrup; refrigerate.

To make punch: In large punch bowl, combine grapefruit juice, 1½ cups syrup and seltzer; add ice ring or ice cubes, grapefruit slices and mint leaves.

YIELD: 12 servings (about 8 cups).

Photograph, opposite page.

Tallahassee Tall One, top, page 15; T.G.I. Florida (pitcher); Everglade Punch, right; Carrot Cooler, middle right, page 18; The Maiden Mary, page 19

CARROT COOLER

½   cup Florida grapefruit juice
⅓   cup carrot juice
¼   teaspoon celery salt
    Crushed ice
    Carrot stick or celery stick

Mix together grapefruit juice, carrot juice and celery salt until smooth; pour over ice in wide, short glass or glass mug.

Garnish with carrot and/or celery sticks.

YIELD: 1 serving.

Photograph, page 17, middle right.

A sweet combination of three fruits.

KEY WEST KOOLER

1½   cups Florida grapefruit juice
1   small, ripe banana, cut into chunks
1   kiwi fruit, peeled and sliced
1   tablespoon honey
1   cup ice cubes
     Rum or vodka (optional)
     Wedges of Florida grapefruit

In container of electric blender, combine grapefruit juice, banana, kiwi, honey and ice. Cover. Blend at high speed until smooth and frothy. (Rum or vodka can be added, if desired.) Pour into large, iced dacquiri glasses.

Garnish with wedge of grapefruit.

YIELD: 2 servings.

Photograph, page 17, bottom.

THE MAIDEN MARY

2½	*cups Florida grapefruit juice*
2	*cups tomato juice*
1	*cup clam juice*
2	*teaspoons Worcestershire sauce*
	Dash hot pepper sauce
	Ice cubes
4	*scallions*

In a 2-quart pitcher, combine grapefruit juice, tomato juice, clam juice, Worcestershire and hot pepper sauce; blend well. Add ice cubes. Pour into serving glasses.

Garnish with whole scallions.

YIELD: 4 servings.

Photograph, page 17, left.

Spiced and mulled drinks have hundreds of years of tradition behind them.

HOT SPICED CITRUS TEA

2	*cups water*
4	*tea bags*
3	*whole cloves*
1	*cinnamon stick, 3 inches long*
1	*cup Florida orange juice*
1	*cup Florida grapefruit juice*
3	*tablespoons butter or margarine (optional)*
½	*cup light rum (optional)*
5 to 8	*tablespoons sugar (to taste)*

In a medium saucepan, bring water to a boil. Remove from heat. Add tea bags and spices; cover, brew 5 minutes. Remove tea bags and spices. Add orange juice and grapefruit juice. Heat through but do not boil. Remove from heat.

Add butter and rum if desired, stirring until butter melts. Add sugar to taste.

YIELD: 4 to 6 servings.

MULLED GRAPEFRUIT TODDY

3	cups Florida grapefruit juice
3	cups apple juice
3	cups white grape juice
18	whole cloves
3	cinnamon sticks
⅓	cup sugar
⅓	cup brandy (optional)

In large saucepan, combine grapefruit juice, apple juice, grape juice, cloves, cinnamon sticks and sugar. Bring to a boil. Cover. Let steep 5 minutes; strain. Stir in brandy, if desired. Serve hot.

YIELD: 18 (4-ounce) servings.

ORANGE DEVIL

¾	cup Florida orange juice
2	ounces vodka
1	ounce Amaretto liqueur
	Shaved or crushed ice
	Orange slices

Mix together orange juice, vodka and liqueur. Pour over ice in old-fashioned glasses.

Garnish with orange slices.

YIELD: 2 servings.

A recipe for shrub was found in an English cookbook dated 1851. Shrub comes from the Arabic "shurb," meaning drink.

ORANGE SHRUB

5 or 6	Florida oranges
1	quart rum or brandy
1	cup sugar

Squeeze juice from oranges to make 2 cups; strain juice. Reserve. Coarsely chop remains of 2½ oranges. In small saucepan, combine chopped orange and enough water to cover. Cover pan, bring water to boiling. Drain, rinse orange with cold water.

In large bottle, combine strained orange juice, rum, sugar and chopped orange. Cover; shake well. After 8 hours, strain and discard chopped orange. Cover; store at room temperature 4 days. Shake occasionally.

Serve over ice in old-fashioned glasses.

YIELD: About 6½ cups.

FRUIT-BERRY FREEZE

1	cup Florida grapefruit juice
½	cup fresh or frozen strawberries
1 to 2	tablespoons honey
⅔	cup club soda, divided
	Crushed ice
	Fresh strawberries for garnish (optional)

In container of electric blender, combine grapefruit juice, strawberries (except those for garnish) and honey; purée. Pour over ice in 2 tall glasses. Add ⅓ cup club soda to each. Stir.

Garnish with a fresh strawberry, if desired.

YIELD: 2 servings.

Photograph, page 23, right.

Excellent meal-in-itself when time is short in the morning.

ORANGE WAKE-UP DRINK

1	cup Florida orange juice
1	egg
¼	cup nonfat dry milk powder
2	tablespoons wheat germ
1	tablespoon honey
3	ice cubes

In container of electric blender, combine all ingredients. Cover and process at high speed until smooth. Pour into tall glasses.

YIELD: 2 servings.

GOLDEN BREAKFAST NOG

¾	cup Florida orange juice, chilled
¾	cup Florida grapefruit juice, chilled
1	small banana
2	eggs
½	cup vanilla yogurt
1½	tablespoons honey
	Wheat germ

In container of electric blender, combine juice, banana, eggs, yogurt and honey. Cover. Process until smooth. Pour into serving glasses.

Sprinkle each serving with wheat germ.

YIELD: 2 servings.

Photograph, opposite page.

Fruit Berry Freeze, right, page 21; Fresh Melon Slush, front, page 24; Golden Breakfast Nog, left; Setting Sun, back, page 24

A pretty, non-alcoholic party drink.

SETTING SUN

2	teaspoons grenadine
6	tablespoons (½ of 6-ounce can) Florida frozen concentrated orange juice, thawed, undiluted
16	ounces (2 cups) club soda, chilled
	Ice

Spoon grenadine into 2 tulip-shaped glasses or narrow wine glasses. Combine orange juice concentrate and club soda; gently pour down the side of the glass. Add ice. Stir before drinking.

YIELD: 2 servings.

Photograph, page 23, back.

FRESH MELON SLUSH

2	cups melon cubes (cantaloupe, crenshaw, or honeydew)
1	cup milk
6	tablespoons (½ of 6-ounce can) Florida frozen concentrated orange juice, thawed, undiluted
2	cups crushed ice
	Orange slice and 2 melon balls for garnish

In container of electric blender combine all ingredients except orange slice and melon balls for garnish. Process about 30 seconds until slushy. Pour into serving glasses.

Garnish with orange slice and melon balls on a long pick.

YIELD: 3 servings.

Photograph, page 23, front.

GRAPEFRUIT SANGRIA

3	cups Florida grapefruit juice, chilled
1½	cups white grape juice, chilled
1	Florida orange, sliced
1	apple, cored and sliced
1½	cups honeydew melon chunks
1½	cups club soda, cold
	Ice cubes

In large pitcher, combine grapefruit juice, grape juice, orange and apple slices and melon chunks. Add club soda and ice cubes. Stir.

Serve in wine glasses.

YIELD: 6 servings.

One of the oldest Christmas customs is the hot punch, or "wassail."

HOT HOLIDAY PUNCH

1	cup granulated sugar
½	cup packed brown sugar
4	cups apple cider
1	cinnamon stick, 3 inches long
12	whole cloves
2	cups Florida grapefruit juice
2	cups Florida orange juice
	Orange slices
	Maraschino cherry halves
	Whole cloves

In large saucepan, combine granulated sugar, brown sugar and apple cider. Heat, stirring, until sugar dissolves. Add cinnamon stick and cloves. Bring mixture to a boil over medium heat; reduce heat, simmer 5 minutes.

Add grapefruit and orange juice. Heat, but do not boil. Strain. Pour into heat-proof punch bowl.

Garnish with orange slices decorated with maraschino cherry halves and whole cloves. Serve in heat-proof punch cups.

YIELD: 8 servings.

Orange juice and spices make this iced tea a special drink.

ORANGE N' SPICE ICED TEA

6	cups cold water, divided
3	2-inch cinnamon sticks
½	teaspoon whole cloves
10	tea bags
1	can (6 ounces) Florida frozen concentrated orange juice, thawed, undiluted
¼	cup sugar
1	Florida orange, sliced

In medium saucepan, combine 3 cups cold water, cinnamon sticks and cloves. Bring to boiling; remove from heat, add tea bags. Brew 5 minutes. Remove tea bags, discard. Strain mixture. Add remaining 3 cups cold water, orange juice concentrate and sugar; mix well. Chill. Serve in tall glasses over ice cubes.

Garnish with fresh orange slices.

YIELD: 6 (8-ounce) servings.

GRAPEFRUIT COCO PUNCH

6	cups Florida grapefruit juice, chilled
¾	cup canned cream of coconut
1	quart club soda, chilled
	Ice cubes

In punch bowl, combine grapefruit juice and cream of coconut; blend well. Add club soda and ice cubes. Mix and serve.

YIELD: 2½ quarts.

TANGERINE ISLAND SHAKE

1   can (6 ounces) Florida frozen concentrated tangerine juice, thawed, undiluted
2   cups milk
1½   cups vanilla ice cream
      Flaked coconut (optional)

Combine tangerine juice concentrate, milk and ice cream in container of electric blender. Cover. Process at high speed 10 seconds or until smooth. Pour into tall glasses.

Garnish with flaked coconut, if desired.

YIELD: 4 (8-ounce) servings.

A popular wedding and party punch.

CRYSTAL ORANGE PUNCH

3   cups boiling water
2   tablespoons loose tea or 6 tea bags
4   tablespoons snipped mint leaves
½   cup light corn syrup
3   cans (6 ounces each) Florida frozen concentrated orange juice, thawed, undiluted
¼   cup lime juice
1   pint orange sherbet, softened
2   bottles (750 ML. each) champagne
4   cups ice cubes
2   Florida oranges, sliced
6   strawberries, sliced

Bring water to a full boil in saucepan. Remove from heat and immediately add tea and mint leaves. Brew, uncovered, 4 minutes. Stir and strain into large bowl or pitcher; cool. Stir in corn syrup, undiluted orange juice concentrate, lime juice and sherbet. Just before serving, pour into punch bowl over ice cubes; add champagne.

Garnish with orange and strawberry slices.

YIELD: Approximately 40 (½-cup) servings.

Soups, Salads and Breads

Soups, Salads and Breads

Soups, salads and breads for generations have been staples of eating and entertainment. These dishes were once ho-hum and predictable. What a difference a new generation makes! Citrus in today's lifestyle has elevated soups, salads and breads to an exciting new status.

Grated citrus peel and citrus juices enliven any hot soup, giving it a special tang and richness. Citrus delightfully accents the fresh, natural flavors of cold soups and fruit soups, becoming more and more popular the year 'round. A citrus garnish adds a colorful gourmet touch to soups.

With the present emphasis on enjoyable and healthy eating, citrus is a welcome part of many salads and salad dressings. As a main dish, today's innovative salad is often a meal in itself. Lighter salads, too, feature stimulating ingredients. Citrus juices, sections and peel make all salads better.

Breads enjoy a greater range of uses than ever before. Served at meals, for snacks, as gifts, breads featuring citrus peel and juices provide enticing aromas and irresistible tastes.

Soups, salads and breads are here to stay, not only because they are well loved, but also because they are better than ever—and much of the thanks goes to citrus.

Opening photograph: Fish Soup Sarasota, top left, page 31; Winter Haven Salad, bottom left, page 41; Orange Date and Nut Bread, right, page 59

With its variety of garnishes, this soup makes a very good buffet offering.

FISH SOUP SARASOTA

2	tablespoons vegetable oil
1	cup sliced celery
1	large onion, sliced (1 cup)
2	cloves garlic, sliced
2	pounds fish bones or heads
1	quart water
10	peppercorns
1	teaspoon dried leaf thyme, crumbled
¾	teaspoon salt
½	teaspoon fennel seeds
1½	pounds halibut, cod or haddock, cut in 1-inch chunks
1½	cups Florida grapefruit juice
1	cup bottled clam juice
	Assorted Garnishes: Grated Parmesan cheese, chopped parsley, cooked pasta, garlic croutons, cooked shellfish, chopped tomatoes, sliced black olives

In large pot or heavy kettle, heat oil; sauté celery, onion and garlic until tender. Add fish bones, water, peppercorns, thyme, salt and fennel seeds; bring to a boil. Cover. Reduce heat; simmer 30 minutes.

Skim off "scum" that rises to the top. Strain broth through a sieve. Return broth to pot.

Add fish chunks, grapefruit juice and clam juice. Simmer 10 minutes until fish is cooked. Serve with assorted garnishes.

YIELD: 8 to 10 servings.

Photograph, page 28.

DANISH BUTTERMILK SOUP

6   egg yolks
¼   cup sugar
1   quart buttermilk
6   tablespoons (½ of a 6-ounce can) Florida frozen
         concentrated grapefruit juice, thawed,
         undiluted
       Daisy flower (optional)

In large bowl of electric mixer, beat egg yolks and sugar until thick and lemon-colored. Gently stir in buttermilk and grapefruit juice concentrate. Chill.

Garnish with daisy flower.

YIELD: 4 servings (about 5 cups).

Photograph, opposite page.

ORANGE-RASPBERRY SOUP

2   cups light cream or half-and-half
1   package (10 ounces) frozen raspberries, thawed
1   can (6 ounces) Florida frozen concentrated orange
         juice, thawed, undiluted
½   cup heavy cream, whipped
       Grated orange peel

In container of electric blender, combine light cream, raspberries and orange juice concentrate. Cover. Process on high 1 minute until smooth. Chill.

Garnish with whipped cream and sprinkle with grated orange peel.

YIELD: 4 servings (about 5 cups).

Photograph, opposite page.

Orange Cantaloupe Soup, top, page 35; Danish Buttermilk Soup, right; Orange Raspberry Soup, left; Sunshine Avocado Soup, bottom, page 34

SUNSHINE AVOCADO SOUP

2	cups light cream or half-and-half
1¼	cups water
1	can (6 ounces) Florida frozen concentrated orange juice, thawed, undiluted
2	ripe avocados
½	teaspoon salt
⅛	teaspoon hot pepper sauce
4	Florida orange slices

In container of electric blender, combine light cream, water and orange juice concentrate. Process until smooth.

Peel and seed avocados. Cut 1½ avocados into chunks. Add to blender with salt and hot pepper sauce. Blend 1 minute until smooth. Chill.

Cut remaining avocado half into slices. Garnish soup with avocado and orange slices.

YIELD: 4 servings (about 5 cups).

Photograph, page 33, bottom.

ORANGE FRUIT SOUP

3	cans (16 ounces each) pears, drained
6	cups Florida orange juice
1½	teaspoons ground cardamom
¾	cup sour cream
5	Florida oranges, peeled and sectioned
	Assorted Garnishes: Toasted coconut, avocado slices, macadamia nuts, orange and grapefruit sections

Purée pears in blender until smooth. (This may be done in several batches.) Pour purée into a bowl. Stir in orange juice, cardamom and sour cream. Chill. Add orange sections.

Serve with assorted garnishes.

YIELD: 8 to 10 servings.

ORANGE CANTALOUPE SOUP

1	large cantaloupe
2	cups water, divided
1	can (6 ounces) Florida frozen concentrated orange juice, thawed, undiluted
½	teaspoon salt
⅛	teaspoon ground cinnamon
	Dash mace
2	tablespoons cornstarch

Cut cantaloupe in half, remove seeds. Using a melon-ball scoop, scoop balls from one half; set aside. Scrape out remaining pulp; reserve. Peel remaining half; cut into chunks. Place cantaloupe chunks and pulp in container of electric blender; cover; process until smooth. (You should have 1 cup purée.) Add 1 cup water, orange juice concentrate , salt, cinnamon and mace. Cover. Process 5 seconds. Remove to bowl.

In small saucepan, combine cornstarch and remaining 1 cup water; stir to dissolve cornstarch. Cook over medium heat until mixture boils and thickens. Gently stir into cantaloupe mixture. Add melon balls. Cover. Chill well before serving.

YIELD: 4 servings (about 5 cups).

Photograph, page 33, top.

A curry dish is a recommended entrée with this soup.

ROYAL CARROT SOUP

3	cups chicken broth
2	cups Florida grapefruit juice
6 to 8	medium carrots (1 pound) pared, cut in chunks
1	medium onion, cut in chunks
¾	teaspoon ground cumin
½	teaspoon ground cinnamon
¼	teaspoon salt
1	cup sour cream or plain yogurt

In large saucepan, combine broth, grapefruit juice, carrots, onion, cumin, cinnamon and salt. Bring to a boil. Reduce heat. Simmer 25 minutes or until carrots are tender. Purée vegetables and cooking liquid in a blender or food processor. Return to saucepan; heat. Serve with sour cream or yogurt.

YIELD: 6 servings (about 8 cups).

CHILLED CUCUMBER SOUP

This soup is good on picnics, as well as a light first course for a formal meal.

4   large cucumbers, pared, seeded, cut in pieces (6 cups)
1   can (6 ounces) Florida frozen concentrated grapefruit juice, thawed, undiluted
6   cups chicken broth or bouillon, degreased
1   cup sliced dill pickles, drained
2   small scallions
2   teaspoons dried leaf tarragon
2   cups dry champagne or dry white wine, chilled
1   cup sour cream

Combine cucumber, grapefruit juice concentrate, chicken broth, pickles, scallions and tarragon. Cover. Process in blender or food processor, in several batches, until smooth. Chill at least 1 hour.

Just before serving, stir in champagne. Serve with sour cream.

YIELD: 8 servings (about 10 cups).

FIVE FRUIT SOUP

With this example to inspire you, try other fruit combinations, using grapefruit juice to blend the flavors.

2   cups Florida grapefruit juice
1   cup Florida orange juice
1   cup buttermilk
1   ripe banana, cut in chunks
1   cup sliced, fresh strawberries
1   cup cantaloupe pieces
2   teaspoons sugar
½   teaspoon ground cardamom
    Strawberries and fresh mint for garnish (optional)

Combine all ingredients (except strawberries and mint for garnish), in several batches, in a container of electric blender or food processor; cover; blend until smooth.

Chill at least 1 hour.

Garnish with strawberry slices and fresh mint, if desired.

YIELD: 4 servings (about 6 cups).

A yogurt dressing spiked with coriander and ginger is the finishing touch to a splendid vegetable salad.

WINTER CITRUS SALAD

2   *cups fresh broccoli flowerets*
1½   *cups thinly sliced fresh carrots*
3   *cups Florida grapefruit sections*
     Florida grapefruit juice, drained from sections, approximately ½ cup
1½   *cups drained chick peas*
⅓   *cup raisins*
1   *cup broken walnuts*

In medium saucepan, cook broccoli and carrots in 1-inch boiling, salted water 3 minutes. Drain. Return vegetables to saucepan, add grapefruit sections, juice, chick peas and raisins; heat 1 minute.

Spoon into serving bowl. Add walnuts; mix gently. Serve warm with Yogurt Dressing*.

YIELD: 4 servings.

*YOGURT DRESSING

1   *cup plain yogurt*
¼   *cup mayonnaise*
2   *tablespoons chopped scallions*
1   *tablespoon honey*
1¼   *teaspoons ground coriander*
1¼   *teaspoons ground ginger*
¾   *teaspoon salt*

In medium bowl, combine all ingredients; mix well.

YIELD: About 1⅓ cups.

Photograph, page 39.

GRAPEFRUIT SEAFOOD SALAD

¼	cup salad oil
2	large cloves garlic, minced
2	cups green beans, cut in 1-inch pieces
1	pound scallops
2	cups Florida grapefruit sections
	Florida grapefruit juice, drained from sections, approximately ⅓ cup
3	tablespoons vinegar
¾	teaspoon crushed fennel seeds
¼	teaspoon salt
½	cup sliced, pitted black olives

In medium skillet, heat oil; cook garlic until golden. Add green beans; stir-fry 2 to 3 minutes until crisp-tender. Remove with slotted spoon to a large bowl.

In same skillet, stir-fry scallops 2 to 3 minutes until done. Remove with slotted spoon and add to green beans.

Add grapefruit juice to skillet. Stir in vinegar, fennel seeds and salt. Boil mixture, uncovered, until reduced to ⅓ cup. Return beans and scallops to skillet. Add grapefruit sections and olives; toss lightly. Serve immediately.

YIELD: 4 servings.

Photograph, opposite page.

Palm Beach Chicken Salad, top, page 40; Winter Citrus Salad, center, page 37; Grapefruit Seafood Salad, bottom

Main dish salads are perfect examples of the trend toward lightness with robust goodness that satisfies.

PALM BEACH CHICKEN SALAD

½	cup chicken broth
2	whole chicken breasts, boned and skinned
1½	cups uncooked pasta (rotelle, shells, etc.)
1	cup peas, cooked, drained
½	cup pimiento, diced
2	cups Florida grapefruit sections
	Florida grapefruit juice, drained from sections, approximately ⅓ cup
¼	cup salad oil
2	tablespoons wine vinegar
1	large clove garlic, minced
½	teaspoon ground cumin
½	teaspoon salt
⅛	teaspoon white pepper

In medium skillet, bring broth to a boil. Arrange chicken breasts in single layer in pan; return broth to boiling. Cover. Cook about 10 minutes, until chicken is cooked through. Drain. Cut chicken into strips.

Meanwhile, cook pasta according to package directions. Drain.

In large bowl, combine chicken, pasta, peas, pimiento, grapefruit sections and juice.

In small bowl or jar, combine oil, vinegar, garlic, cumin, salt and pepper; mix well. Pour dressing over chicken mixture; toss lightly. Serve warm.

YIELD: 4 servings.

Photograph, page 39.

ORANGE PECAN SLAW

1	small head green or red cabbage, shredded (about 12 cups), or red and green cabbage mixed
1	cup chopped pecans
4	Florida oranges, peeled and diced
¾	cup bottled slaw dressing
1	tablespoon lemon juice
1	tablespoon honey
½	teaspoon salt (optional)

In large mixing bowl, combine cabbage, pecans and orange pieces.

In small bowl or jar, combine slaw dressing, lemon juice, honey and salt; stir or shake to blend well. Pour dressing over slaw. Toss lightly. Cover. Chill 1 hour.

YIELD: 6 to 8 servings.

WINTER HAVEN SALAD

2	Florida pink grapefruit, peeled and sectioned (2 cups sections)
2	small red onions, thinly sliced and separated into rings
1	pound fresh green beans, trimmed, cooked, drained
1	can (1 pound) artichoke hearts, drained, cut in halves
	Lettuce leaves
¾	cup salad oil
⅓	cup tarragon wine vinegar
1	clove garlic, finely minced
½	teaspoon salt
¼	teaspoon pepper

Arrange grapefruit sections, onions, green beans and artichoke hearts on lettuce-lined serving plates.

In small bowl or jar, combine oil, vinegar, garlic, salt and pepper; mix well. Serve dressing with salad.

YIELD: 4 to 6 servings.

Photograph, page 28.

One tangelo, tangerine, or a combination of both make a pretty grapefruit substitute.

GOLD COAST SALAD

	Lettuce leaves
1	pound shrimp, cooked, peeled, deveined
2	Florida oranges, peeled, sliced
1	Florida grapefruit, peeled, sliced
2	medium tomatoes, cut in wedges
1	red Bell pepper, seeded, sliced
1	avocado, peeled, cut in wedges
½	cup sliced celery
½	cup pitted black olives

Arrange lettuce leaves on a serving plate. Arrange remaining ingredients on lettuce.

Serve with Gold Coast Salad Dressing*.

YIELD: 4 servings.

*GOLD COAST SALAD DRESSING

1	cup sour cream
2	tablespoons Florida frozen concentrated orange juice, thawed, undiluted
1	tablespoon Dijon-style mustard
2	teaspoons prepared horseradish
2	scallions, finely chopped

In small bowl, combine sour cream, orange juice concentrate, mustard, and horseradish; fold in chopped scallions. Cover. Chill about one hour.

YIELD: 1¼ cups dressing.

Photograph, opposite page.

Gold Coast Salad

SUNBURST SALAD

4	cups cooked pasta shells
3	Florida pink grapefruit, peeled and sectioned (reserve juice for dressing)
1	cup sliced celery
½	cup sliced carrots
½	cup peas, cooked
½	cup chopped parsley
¼	cup chopped green onions
½	cup salad oil
⅓	cup Florida grapefruit juice
2	tablespoons distilled white vinegar
1	teaspoon dried dill weed, crumbled
1	teaspoon celery seed
½	teaspoon salt
1	can (15 ounces) pink salmon, drained
	Lettuce

In large bowl, combine pasta shells, grapefruit sections, celery, carrots, peas, parsley and green onions.

In screw-top jar, combine oil, grapefruit juice, vinegar, dill, celery seed and salt. Shake well. Pour dressing over pasta mixture. Toss well. Cover. Chill 30 minutes.

Break salmon into large pieces, fold into pasta mixture. To serve, spoon salad onto lettuce-lined plates.

YIELD: 8 servings.

Very good with chicken, ham, pork or fish.

ORANGE SALAD MARRAKESH

4   *Florida oranges, peeled, sliced*
½   *cup thinly sliced radishes*
⅓   *cup sliced, pitted black olives*
¼   *cup Florida grapefruit juice*
¼   *teaspoon ground cinnamon*

In a shallow bowl, combine oranges, radishes and olives. Combine grapefruit juice and cinnamon; pour over orange mixture. Cover. Chill 2 to 3 hours.

Serve on bed of lettuce.

YIELD: 4 servings.

Attractive on a buffet table accompanied by Sally Lunn Bread, page 53.

8-LAYER SALAD

½   *cup mayonnaise*
½   *cup plain yogurt*
1½   *cups shredded lettuce*
1   *large tomato, diced (1 cup)*
2   *Florida grapefruit, peeled and sectioned*
2   *scallions, chopped (¾ cup)*
1   *can (16 ounces) red kidney beans, drained*
4   *ounces Feta cheese, crumbled (½ cup)*
½   *pound snow peas (1 cup), cooked until crisp-tender*
3   *Florida Valencia oranges, peeled and sectioned*
1   *scallion, chopped, for garnish (optional)*

In a small bowl, combine mayonnaise and yogurt; mix well. In a 2-quart, straight-sided glass bowl, arrange layers of lettuce, tomato, grapefruit sections, scallions, kidney beans, cheese and snow peas.

Spread mayonnaise mixture over all. Arrange orange sections on top. Sprinkle with additional chopped scallions, if desired. Cover. Chill 4 to 6 hours before serving.

YIELD: 8 servings.

SPINACH SALAD A LA FLORIDA

¾   cup blue cheese, crumbled (about ¼ pound)
½   cup salad oil
¼   cup Florida grapefruit juice
½   teaspoon seasoned salt
1   cup sour cream
6   cups fresh spinach, washed, drained and broken into
        bite-size pieces
6   Florida oranges, peeled and sectioned
½   cup cashews

In container of electric blender, combine blue cheese, salad oil, grapefruit juice and seasoned salt. Cover. Blend until smooth. Or, use a small bowl and an electric mixer.

Stir in sour cream. Cover. Chill at least 1 hour to blend flavors.

Meanwhile, prepare spinach and oranges. Just before serving, combine spinach, oranges, cashews and dressing.

YIELD: 6 to 8 servings.

Truly an example of exotic fare made by combining everyday ingredients in an unusual fashion.

INDONESIAN RICE SALAD

2   cups cooked brown rice
3   Florida oranges, peeled, sectioned
½   cup raisins
½   cup chopped scallions
½   cup sliced celery
½   cup sliced water chestnuts
¼   cup toasted sesame seeds

In large bowl, combine all ingredients; mix well. Serve chilled or at room temperature. Serve with Soy-Citrus Dressing*.

YIELD: 6 servings.   *continued*

SOY-CITRUS DRESSING

⅓   cup Florida orange juice
¼   cup vegetable oil
2   tablespoons soy sauce

In small bowl, combine all ingredients; mix well.

YIELD: About ¾ cup.

Add the important element of color to your meal with this salad.

BEET AND ORANGE SALAD

½   cup vegetable oil
¼   cup white wine vinegar
¼   cup chopped scallions
1   clove garlic, minced
2½   teaspoons ground coriander
½   teaspoon salt
⅛   teaspoon pepper
2   Florida oranges, peeled and sliced
1   can (1 pound) julienne beets, drained
½   cup broken walnuts
1   bunch watercress, washed

In medium bowl, combine oil, vinegar, scallions, garlic, coriander, salt and pepper; mix well.

In small bowl, combine orange slices, and half the marinade mixture. Cover. Chill overnight.

In another small bowl, combine beets and remaining marinade mixture. Cover. Chill overnight.

To serve, drain oranges and beets. Combine oranges, beets and walnuts and serve on bed of watercress.

YIELD: 4 to 6 servings.

Pasta shells are delicate and tender, vegetables lend crispness, while orange sections add succulence and sweet fragrance to the dish.

ORANGE PRIMAVERA SALAD

2	cups cooked baby shell pasta, chilled
2	cups broccoli flowerets, blanched
1	carrot, sliced, blanched
¼	pound snow peas, washed, trimmed and cut in half lengthwise
½	cup red Bell peppers, julienned
6	Florida oranges, peeled and sectioned

In large bowl, combine pasta, broccoli, carrot slices, snow peas and red pepper. Toss well with Fresh As Spring Dressing*. Chill.

Slice 2 oranges, cut each slice in half and arrange round side up along the sides of a 2-inch-deep serving dish.

Spoon salad into dish.

YIELD: 6 servings.

*FRESH AS SPRING DRESSING

4	teaspoons vinegar
1	tablespoon prepared mustard
1	egg yolk
½	teaspoon dried dill weed
1	small clove garlic, minced
⅛	teaspoon salt
⅛	teaspoon hot pepper sauce
⅓	cup olive oil

In small bowl, combine vinegar, mustard, egg yolk, dill weed, garlic, salt and hot pepper sauce. Using fork or wire whisk, quickly blend in olive oil until mixture is smooth.

YIELD: About ½ cup.

Photograph, opposite page.

Orange Primavera Salad

GRAPEFRUIT SALAD MIRAMAR

2	cups water
1	bay leaf
½	teaspoon salt
2	lemon slices
1	pound scallops
1	cup green beans, cut in 2-inch pieces, cooked, drained
1	cup yellow beans, cut in 2-inch pieces, cooked, drained
1	can (8 ounces) red kidney beans, drained
2	Florida grapefruit, peeled and sectioned
1	small red onion, thinly sliced

In a medium saucepan, combine water, bay leaf, salt and lemon slices; bring to boiling. Add scallops; cook 3 minutes. Drain. Cool.

In large bowl, combine scallops with rest of ingredients. Add Grapefruit Vinaigrette*; toss lightly. Cover. Chill 3 to 4 hours before serving, stirring occasionally.

YIELD: 4 to 6 servings.

*GRAPEFRUIT VINAIGRETTE

½	cup Florida grapefruit juice
⅓	cup white wine vinegar
⅓	cup vegetable oil
1	clove garlic, minced
2	tablespoons bottled capers, drained
1	tablespoon Dijon-style mustard
1¼	teaspoons dried leaf tarragon, crumbled
½	teaspoon salt
¼	teaspoon pepper

Combine all ingredients; mix well.

YIELD: About 1¼ cups.

A nice holiday bread.

BISHOP'S BREAD

3	cups packaged biscuit mix
½	cup sugar
1	egg
1	tablespoon grated orange peel
1¼	cups Florida orange juice
3	tablespoons salad oil
½	cup wheat germ
1	6-ounce package (1 cup) semi-sweet chocolate morsels, divided
¼	cup seedless raisins
¼	cup candied cherries, halved
¼	cup chopped nuts

Preheat oven to 350°F.

Combine biscuit mix and sugar in large mixing bowl.

In a separate bowl, combine egg, orange peel, orange juice and salad oil. Add to biscuit mix and beat with wooden spoon until mixture is smooth. Stir in wheat germ, ⅔ cup of chocolate morsels, raisins, cherries and nuts.

Turn into greased 9 x 5 x 3-inch loaf pan. Sprinkle remaining chocolate morsels on top of batter. Bake in 350°F. oven 55 to 60 minutes, until a cake tester in center comes out clean. Let cool in pan 10 minutes. Turn out of pan. Cool completely on wire rack.

YIELD: 1 loaf.

A new twist on a popular Southern recipe.

ORANGE CRACKLING BREAD

½	pound salt pork, cut in cubes
2	tablespoons finely chopped onion
1½	cups yellow cornmeal
½	cup sifted all-purpose flour
3	teaspoons baking powder
1	teaspoon sugar
2	eggs
½	cup buttermilk
1	cup Florida orange juice
1	teaspoon grated orange peel

Preheat oven to 350°F.

In 9-inch oven-proof skillet, cook salt pork over low heat until very crisp, remove and chop finely. Drain all but 1 tablespoon fat; cook onion until tender.

In large bowl, mix together cornmeal, flour, baking powder and sugar.

In small bowl, beat eggs with buttermilk and orange juice; stir in orange peel. Add egg mixture all at once to dry ingredients; stir just until mixed. Stir in salt pork and onion.

Heat skillet in oven 5 minutes or over high heat on top of stove 1 minute; pour in batter. Bake in a 350°F. oven 30 to 35 minutes. Serve hot with butter.

YIELD: 8 servings.

Photograph, page 55.

Orange juice is a special addition to this popular old-fashioned bread.

SALLY LUNN BREAD

1	*package active dry yeast*
¼	*cup warm water*
¾	*cup milk*
¼	*cup sugar*
¼	*cup butter or margarine*
1	*teaspoon grated orange peel*
1	*teaspoon salt*
1	*cup Florida orange juice*
2	*eggs, beaten*
6	*cups sifted all-purpose flour*
2	*Florida oranges, sliced*

In small bowl, dissolve yeast in warm water; set aside. In medium saucepan, scald milk; add sugar, butter, orange peel and salt. Stir until sugar dissolves and butter melts. Cool.

In large bowl, combine milk mixture, yeast, orange juice, eggs and flour. Beat until smooth (dough will be very soft).

Turn into a greased bundt pan or 10-inch tube pan. Let rise in warm place, covered, until doubled in bulk, about 1 hour.

Preheat oven to 400°F.

Bake in a 400°F. oven 15 minutes, reduce oven temperature to 350°F. and bake 15 to 20 minutes longer, or until bread is browned. Cool 5 minutes in pan; turn out on wire rack and cool completely.

Garnish serving platter with orange slices cut in half and surrounding loaf.

YIELD: One loaf.

Photograph, page 55.

A wonderful breakfast or brunch bread.

ORANGE RAISIN BREAD

1	cup dark raisins
1	cup Florida orange juice
1	package active dry yeast
¼	cup warm water
2	large eggs, beaten
⅓	cup butter or margarine, melted
⅓	cup firmly packed brown sugar
2	teaspoons grated orange peel
1	teaspoon salt
½	teaspoon ground cinnamon
5 to 6	cups all-purpose flour

In small bowl, soak raisins in orange juice one hour. In large bowl, combine yeast and warm water; stir until yeast is dissolved. Add raisin and orange juice mixture, eggs, butter, sugar, orange peel, salt and cinnamon. Beat in enough flour to make a soft dough.

Turn out onto floured surface. Knead about 5 minutes, adding flour as necessary until dough is smooth and elastic. Put dough into large greased bowl; turn over to bring greased side up; cover with towel. Let rise in warm place about 1 hour or until doubled in bulk. Punch down dough and turn out on lightly floured board. Knead about 5 minutes, until smooth. Shape into a loaf to fit into a greased 9 x 5-inch loaf pan; cover. Let rise in warm place about 50 minutes or until doubled in bulk.

Preheat oven to 350°F.

Bake in a 350°F. oven 55 to 60 minutes until golden. Cool in pan 5 minutes; remove from pan and cool completely on wire rack.

YIELD: 1 loaf.

Photograph, opposite page.

Sally Lunn Bread, top, page 53; Orange Crackling Bread, middle, page 52; Orange Raisin Bread, bottom

This miniature bread, studded with dark currants, owes its zesty flavor to the orange juice and touch of grated rind.

ORANGE SCONES

2⅔	cups unsifted all-purpose flour
1	teaspoon baking soda
1	teaspoon baking powder
½	teaspoon salt
2	tablespoons sugar
½	cup butter or margarine
1	tablespoon grated orange peel
½	cup currants
3	tablespoons cider vinegar
¾	cup Florida orange juice
1	egg, beaten
	Milk
	Sugar

Preheat oven to 425°F.

In a large mixing bowl, mix flour with baking soda, baking powder, salt and sugar. Cut in butter with two knives or pastry blender until mixture resembles coarse corn meal. Stir in grated orange peel and currants.

Combine vinegar and orange juice in a small bowl. Make a well in center of flour mixture; add juice and egg all at once. Stir mixture with a fork until all dry ingredients are moistened.

Turn onto a floured board; knead gently 8 to 10 times, adding a little more flour if necessary.

Roll into a 12 x 6-inch rectangle. Cut into eight 3-inch squares; cut each square in half diagonally to make two triangles. Brush tops with milk; sprinkle with sugar. Place on greased baking sheets. Bake in a 425°F. oven about 15 minutes or until golden brown.

YIELD: 16 scones.

ORANGE PECAN BREAD

1¾	cups all-purpose flour
¾	cup sugar
1	teaspoon baking powder
½	teaspoon baking soda
½	teaspoon salt
¾	cup Florida orange juice
1	large egg, lightly beaten
2	tablespoons butter or margarine, melted and cooled
1	tablespoon grated fresh orange peel
½	teaspoon almond extract
½	cup chopped pitted dates
½	cup chopped pecans

Preheat oven to 350°F.

In a large bowl, mix together flour, sugar, baking powder, baking soda and salt. In a separate bowl, combine orange juice, egg, butter, orange peel and almond extract.

Make a well in center of dry ingredients and drop in orange juice mixture; stir until just combined; stir in dates and pecans.

Turn batter into a greased 9 x 5 x 3-inch loaf pan. Bake in a 350°F. oven 50 minutes or until a cake tester inserted in center comes out clean. Cool in pan 10 minutes. Turn out of pan. Cool completely on wire rack.

YIELD: 1 loaf.

ORANGE AND HONEY MUFFINS

1¼	cups all-purpose flour
¾	cup whole wheat flour
1	teaspoon baking powder
1	teaspoon ground cinnamon
¾	teaspoon baking soda
¼	teaspoon salt
½	cup butter or margarine, at room temperature
½	cup sugar
¼	cup honey
2	large eggs
1½	teaspoons grated orange peel
½	cup Florida orange juice
½	cup raisins
¾	cup chopped walnuts

Preheat oven to 400°F.

In a large bowl, stir flours, baking powder, cinnamon, baking soda and salt together. In another large bowl, cream butter, sugar and honey together until light and fluffy. Beat in eggs, one at a time; add orange peel.

Stir in flour mixture alternately with orange juice until just combined. Do not overmix. Gently fold in raisins and nuts.

Spoon mixture evenly into 12 greased 2½-inch muffin cups. Bake in a 400°F. oven 15 minutes or until a cake tester inserted in the center of one muffin comes out clean.

Remove muffin tin or tins to wire racks. Cool 5 minutes before removing muffins from cups; finish cooling on rack. Serve warm or cool completely and store in an airtight container at room temperature.

YIELD: 12 muffins.

ORANGE DATE AND NUT BREAD

The Chapter's opening photograph features this bread. The combination of foods pictured with the bread makes an excellent light meal.

2½	cups plus 2 tablespoons sifted all-purpose flour, divided
4	teaspoons baking powder
¼	teaspoon salt
¾	cup butter or margarine
¾	cup sugar
3	large eggs
1¼	cups Florida orange juice
1	teaspoon grated orange peel
1½	cups chopped pitted dates
1½	cups chopped walnuts

Preheat oven to 350°F.

Sift together 2½ cups flour, baking powder and salt. In large mixing bowl, beat butter and sugar until light and fluffy. Beat in eggs, one at a time.

Combine orange juice and orange peel; add to creamed mixture alternately with flour mixture, beginning and ending with dry ingredients. Toss dates and nuts with remaining 2 tablespoons flour; fold into batter.

Turn into a greased and floured 9 x 5 x 3-inch loaf pan. Bake in a 350°F. oven 1 hour and 10 minutes or until cake tester inserted in center of bread comes out clean. Cool 10 minutes in pan. Turn out on wire rack; cool completely, top side up.

YIELD: 1 loaf.

Photograph, page 29.

Entrées

Entrées

Citrus is so flexible, so readily available in fruit and juice form, it can heighten the flavor and aroma of all your entrées. Just add grated citrus peel, a few colorful slices of fresh fruit or a cup of citrus juice to your favorite main dish. Stand back and watch the excitement. You have conjured a wizard of a meal that will have family and friends applauding in admiration.

Roast Duckling with Orange Sauce, the opening recipe in this chapter, has long been a cherished mainstay of the classical French repertoire. You will discover that a touch of orange, grapefruit, tangerine or tangelo also adds enchantment to chicken, turkey and hearty game birds.

Citrus rounds out the character of robust sauces and meat dishes. See how beautifully it complements pork, lamb and any number of stews and casseroles.

Seafood is the shape-up favorite of today's calorie-conscious generation. Steam, poach or broil fresh fish and shellfish. You will be amazed how a dash of citrus subtly accentuates the delicate tastes and aromas.

Chinese, Mexican, Middle Eastern, Italian—citrus also does wonders for ethnic entrées.

Your main dish deserves the best. Be adventurous. Add the flair of citrus.

Opening photograph: Roast Duckling
with Orange Sauce, page 63

Today's duckling is flavorful and tender due to careful breeding. It is also easy to prepare. Serve as a family treat or for a special occasion.

ROAST DUCKLING WITH ORANGE SAUCE

2	ducklings, 4 to 5 pounds each
1	teaspoon salt
1½	cups Florida orange juice, divided
½	cup honey

Preheat oven to 350° F.

Rinse ducklings and pat dry. Sprinkle ducklings inside and out with salt. Close cavity with skewers; truss legs. Pierce duckling skin with a fork in several places around the perimeter of the breast and on the back.

Place on rack in roasting pan. Roast in a 350° F. oven 2 to 2½ hours (meat thermometer inserted on inside of thigh should read 170° F. when done.) Use 1 cup orange juice to brush ducklings during roasting. Combine honey with remaining ½ cup orange juice; baste ducklings with honey glaze during last 30 minutes of roasting.

Remove ducklings to heated serving platter, keep warm. Serve with Orange Sauce*.

YIELD: 6 to 8 servings.

*ORANGE SAUCE

1	cup pan drippings from duckling
1½	cups Florida orange juice
3	tablespoons cornstarch
2	teaspoons grated orange peel
4	Florida oranges, peeled and sectioned

To prepare sauce, drain off all fat from pan drippings (there should be about 1 cup drippings.) Combine cornstarch with orange juice. Pour into pan drippings. Add grated peel. Bring to a boil. Simmer 2 minutes until gravy thickens, stirring constantly. Strain. Stir in orange sections. Serve with ducklings.

YIELD: About 2 cups

Photograph, page 60.

In this dish, as in many native Mexican entrées, fruit, particularly oranges, is used to contrast taste and texture.

CHICKEN OLÉ

2	tablespoons vegetable oil
1	large onion, chopped (1 cup)
2	cloves garlic, minced
1	can (10½ ounces) tomato purée
1	cup Florida orange juice
3	tablespoons chopped canned green chilies
1	teaspoon grated orange peel
1	teaspoon ground cinnamon
½	teaspoon dried leaf thyme, crumbled
½	teaspoon salt
1	whole chicken, 3 to 4 pounds
	Salt and pepper
8	new potatoes
3	medium-size red Bell peppers, seeded and thickly sliced

Preheat oven to 350° F.

In large skillet, heat oil; sauté onion and garlic until tender. Add tomato purée, orange juice, chilies, orange peel, cinnamon, thyme and salt. Cook 10 minutes, stirring occasionally.

Meanwhile, sprinkle chicken, inside and out, with salt and pepper. Place chicken in a large casserole or baking dish. Pare a narrow strip around each potato. Arrange potatoes around chicken. Pour sauce over all.

Cover. Bake in a 350° F. oven 45 minutes. Add red peppers; cover; cook 45 minutes longer until chicken and potatoes are tender.

YIELD: 4 servings.

CITRUS CHICKEN IBERIA

1	chicken (about 3 pounds), cut in quarters
2	tablespoons flour
½	teaspoon salt
⅛	teaspoon pepper
2	tablespoons butter or margarine
2	tablespoons olive oil
1	clove garlic, minced
1	can (6 ounces) Florida frozen concentrated orange juice, thawed, undiluted
½	cup chicken broth or water
1	teaspoon dried leaf oregano
1	green pepper, cut in strips
1	red onion, sliced
½	pound mushrooms, sliced
½	cup black olives, sliced

Wash chicken, pat dry. Combine flour, salt and pepper; dredge chicken in flour mixture.

In large skillet, heat butter and oil; sauté garlic until lightly browned. Add chicken and brown on both sides.

Combine orange juice concentrate, chicken broth and oregano; pour over chicken. Cover. Cook 15 minutes. Baste chicken with pan juices.

Add green pepper and onion; cover, cook 5 minutes longer. Add mushrooms and black olives; cover, cook 5 minutes or until chicken is tender.

YIELD: 4 servings.

Serve with Orange Almond Rice, page 122, snow peas and canned water chestnuts, drained and sliced. Steam vegetables three to five minutes.

MOON GATE ORANGE CHICKEN

2	Florida oranges
4	green onions, cut in ¼-inch long pieces
⅓	cup soy sauce
¼	cup sugar
1	cup Florida orange juice
	Vegetable oil for deep frying
3	pounds boned, skinned chicken breasts and thighs, cut in bite-size pieces
2	tablespoons vegetable oil
1	tablespoon shredded fresh ginger or 1 teaspoon ground ginger
¼	teaspoon hot pepper sauce

Score peel of 1 orange in quarter sections; remove peel. Remove all white membrane from peel; cut peel into long, thin strips. Peel second orange; section both oranges. Reserve sections and orange peel strips.

Combine green onions, soy sauce, sugar and orange juice in small bowl; set aside.

Pour oil to depth of 3 inches into large, heavy saucepan. Heat to 375° F. on deep fat thermometer. Fry chicken pieces, a small amount at a time, about 4 minutes or until pieces lose their pink color. Remove with slotted spoon; drain on paper towels.

Heat 2 tablespoons oil in large skillet or wok. Add ginger, hot pepper sauce and orange peel strips; stir-fry 1½ minutes. Add chicken pieces; stir-fry 3 minutes. Add orange juice mixture; stir-fry 3 minutes. Transfer to heated serving dish.

Garnish with orange sections.

YIELD: 8 servings.

Photograph, opposite page.

Orange Almond Rice, page 122; Moongate Orange Chicken

Most of the work in this recipe involves the preparation—mincing, chopping and dicing. If time is short, prepare ingredients ahead of time. Cooking is then quick and easy.

ORANGE CHICKEN ORIENTAL

3	whole broiler-fryer chicken breasts, boned, skinned, and cut into 2-inch pieces
½	teaspoon salt
¼	teaspoon ground ginger
2	tablespoons vegetable oil
1	small garlic clove, minced
1	can (8¼ ounces) pineapple chunks, undrained
1	cup Florida orange juice, divided
1	envelope instant chicken bouillon
2	tablespoons wine vinegar
⅓	cup sliced celery
1	small green pepper, cut into ¼-inch strips
1	small onion, sliced
1	small tomato, cut in wedges
2	tablespoons soy sauce
1	tablespoon sugar
3	tablespoons flour

Sprinkle chicken with salt and ginger.

Heat oil in large skillet, over medium heat; add chicken and garlic and cook 5 minutes. Add liquid from canned pineapple, ¾ cup orange juice, bouillon and vinegar. Cover; simmer 10 minutes.

Add celery, green pepper, and onion. Cover, cook 5 minutes longer. Add tomato wedges and pineapple chunks.

In small bowl, blend together soy sauce, sugar, flour and remaining ¼ cup orange juice. Add to skillet and cook, stirring constantly, until mixture thickens and comes to boiling; cook 1 minute longer.

Serve over hot cooked rice, if desired.

YIELD: 4 servings.

NOTE: To freeze, spoon mixture into freezer bags or containers. To serve, defrost overnight in the refrigerator or for several hours at room temperature. Heat slowly in saucepan; do not boil.

ORANGE-CHESTNUT STUFFED TURKEY

10 to 12	*pound turkey, thawed if frozen, giblets removed*
¼	*cup butter or margarine*
½	*cup chopped celery*
1	*medium onion, chopped (½ cup)*
1	*package (8 ounces) herb seasoned stuffing mix*
3	*cups coarsely chopped, cooked or canned chestnuts*
3	*Florida oranges, peeled, cut in pieces*
1	*cup Florida orange juice, divided*
¼	*cup chopped parsley*
½	*teaspoon salt*
½	*teaspoon dried rosemary*
½	*teaspoon dried leaf thyme, crumbled*

Preheat oven to 325° F.

Rinse turkey; pat dry with paper towels.

In large skillet, melt butter; sauté celery and onion until tender. Stir in stuffing mix, chestnuts, orange pieces, ½ cup orange juice, parsley, salt, rosemary and thyme; mix well. Spoon stuffing loosely into turkey cavity and neck area; close with skewers. Place in a shallow roasting pan, breast-side-up.

Roast in a 325° F. oven 3 to 3½ hours or until a meat thermometer inserted in breast meat registers 185° F. or until juices run clear when the thickest part of the thigh is pierced with a fork.

Baste turkey with remaining ½ cup orange juice and pan drippings during last hour of roasting.

Let turkey rest 20 minutes before carving.

YIELD: 8 to 10 servings.

Photograph, page 119.

Poaching is a quick and easy method of cooking and is practical for one person or a crowd.

CITRUS POACHED CHICKEN BREASTS

1	cup Florida orange juice
¾	cup chicken broth
2	scallions, chopped
2	(6 ounces each) boned, skinned chicken breasts
1½	tablespoons flour
1	bunch watercress
1	Florida orange, peeled and sectioned

In small saucepan, combine orange juice, chicken broth and scallions; simmer 2 minutes. Place chicken breasts in poaching liquid, cover with a piece of wax paper. Simmer slowly 20 to 30 minutes until chicken is cooked through and tender. Remove to heated plate, cover with wax paper and keep warm.

To make sauce, blend ½ cup poaching liquid with flour until smooth. Bring remaining poaching liquid to a boil. While stirring, slowly whisk flour mixture into boiling liquid. Bring to boil and cook until thickened.

Heat water to boiling in a large saucepan. Place watercress in water just long enough to heat, about 15 seconds, drain. Arrange watercress on 2 serving plates as a bed for chicken. Arrange chicken breasts on watercress. Spoon sauce over chicken.

Garnish with orange sections. Serve immediately with remaining sauce on the side.

YIELD: 2 servings.

CHAMPAGNE CHICKEN VALENCIA

When Valencias are not in season, try any in-season orange as a substitute.

½	cup flour
½	teaspoon salt, divided
½	teaspoon pepper, divided
3	whole chicken breasts, skinned, boned and split
¼	cup butter
¼	cup vegetable oil
1½	cups dry champagne or white wine
1	cup Florida orange juice
1	cup heavy cream
4	Florida Valencia oranges, peeled and sectioned

Preheat oven to 350° F.

In small bowl, mix flour with ¼ teaspoon salt and ¼ teaspoon pepper; coat chicken breasts completely with flour mixture.

In large skillet, heat butter and oil; cook chicken until golden brown. Remove from skillet and arrange on a baking sheet. Bake in a 350° F. oven 20 minutes.

Meanwhile, discard excess fat from skillet. Add champagne and orange juice; bring to boiling and reduce liquid by half. Add heavy cream and reduce over high heat until sauce measures about 2 cups.

Place chicken breasts on heated serving platter, top with sauce.

Garnish with orange sections.

YIELD: 6 servings.

An impressive and easy-to-serve entrée, especially suited for dinner parties.

STUFFED CORNISH HENS ORLANDO

3	tablespoons unsalted butter or margarine
¼	cup finely chopped celery
½	cup finely chopped onion
1	clove garlic, minced
1	teaspoon dried leaf tarragon
2	cups whole wheat bread cubes, toasted if desired
1	teaspoon grated orange peel
3	Florida oranges, peeled and sectioned
1	can (8 ounces) water chestnuts, drained, finely chopped
4	Cornish game hens
½	cup Florida orange juice

Preheat oven to 350° F.

In small saucepan, melt butter over medium heat. Sauté celery, onion, garlic and tarragon until onions are translucent.

In large bowl, combine onion mixture, bread cubes, orange peel, orange sections and water chestnuts. Mix well. Stuff each hen lightly with approximately 1 cup stuffing. Place hens in a shallow baking dish. Bake in a 350° F. oven 1 hour or until hens are tender. Baste hens every 15 minutes with orange juice during baking.

YIELD: 4 servings.

Photograph, opposite page.

Braised Pork Chops with Grapefruit, page 94; Orange-Bulgar Vegetarian Casserole, page 101; Stuffed Cornish Hens Orlando

A beautiful presentation for holidays and special occasions. Placed over the ham, the orange slices impart their own succulent flavor while sealing in the moist goodness of the ham.

ORANGE PETAL HAM

10 to 12	*pounds fully-cooked ham, bone-in*
1½	*cups water*
1½	*cups sugar*
5	*Florida oranges, sliced paper thin*
½	*cup brown sugar*
¼	*cup prepared mustard*
½	*teaspoon ground cloves*

Preheat oven to 325°F.

Remove rind from top of ham. Place ham, fat side up, on rack in open, shallow roasting pan. Bake in a 325°F. oven 12 to 15 minutes per pound.

Meanwhile, in medium saucepan, combine water and sugar; bring to a boil. Add orange slices; boil rapidly, uncovered, for 30 minutes. Remove slices from syrup; reserve syrup.

In small bowl, combine brown sugar, mustard and cloves. One half hour before ham is done, remove from oven. Score ham in a diamond pattern. Spread brown sugar mixture over ham. Return to oven and continue baking 10 minutes longer.

Remove from oven; arrange orange slices in rows over ham, overlapping to cover surface completely. Brush slices with reserved syrup. Return to oven and bake 20 minutes longer or until meat thermometer registers 130°F.

YIELD: 8 to 10 servings.

Glazed Sweet Potatoes and Turnips, page 117, makes a very nice accompaniment.

GRAPEFRUIT GLAZED HAM

1   *canned ham (5 to 7 pounds)*
1   *can (6 ounces) Florida frozen concentrated*
        grapefruit juice, thawed, undiluted
     Whole cloves
2   *tablespoons prepared mustard*
½   *cup honey*
½   *teaspoon hot pepper sauce*

Preheat oven to 325°F.

Remove ham from can; place on rack in shallow roasting pan. Bake in 325°F. oven 10 minutes per pound, or follow directions on can for heating. About 15 minutes before end of cooking time, remove from oven.

Score top of ham by making diagonal cuts on top of ham, ⅛-inch deep, about 1 inch apart. Repeat, crossing these lines. Place a whole clove at the point of each diamond.

Make grapefruit glaze by combining grapefruit juice concentrate, prepared mustard, honey and pepper sauce; brush over ham.

Return ham to oven and continue baking 15 minutes, brushing occasionally with glaze.

YIELD: 12 to 16 servings.

Kasha is a grain similar to buckwheat with Asiatic Russian origins.

STUFFED BREAST OF VEAL

¼ cup butter or margarine
1½ cups chopped onion
1 cup chopped celery
2 cloves garlic, minced, divided
2 cups chopped mushrooms
½ cup uncooked kasha
1 egg, lightly beaten
2¾ cups Florida orange juice, divided
½ teaspoon salt
¼ teaspoon dried leaf tarragon, crumbled
5 pounds veal breast, cut with pocket
  Salt
  Pepper
1 large onion, sliced
1 can (8 ounces) tomato sauce
1 Florida orange, sliced
  Parsley

Preheat oven to 350°F.

In large skillet, melt butter; sauté onion, celery and 1 clove garlic 3 minutes. Add mushrooms; cook 2 minutes longer. Combine kasha and egg; stir into vegetable mixture. Add 1¼ cups orange juice, salt and tarragon; mix well. Cover. Cook over low heat about 8 minutes until all liquid is absorbed.

Spoon kasha stuffing into pocket of veal; secure opening with skewers. Place veal in a shallow roasting pan; season with salt and pepper. Place onion slices on top and around veal. Combine remaining garlic, remaining 1½ cups orange juice and tomato sauce; pour over meat.

Roast, uncovered, in a 350°F. oven 2¼ to 2½ hours or until tender, basting with pan juices every 30 minutes. Place roast on heated serving platter.

Garnish with orange slices and parsley. Serve with pan juices.

YIELD: 4 to 6 servings.

CITRUS VEAL MAJORCA

1 to 1½	*pounds veal, scallopini*
4 to 6	*very thin slices mild, cured ham*
2	*Florida oranges, peeled and sectioned*
1	*egg, lightly beaten*
½	*cup milk*
½	*cup fine dry packaged bread crumbs*
1	*teaspoon salt*
½	*teaspoon ground pepper*
6	*tablespoons olive oil*
1	*small onion, chopped*
1	*cup Florida orange juice, divided*
2	*tablespoons cornstarch*
½	*cup dry sherry*
½	*teaspoon grated orange peel*
1	*Florida orange, peeled and sliced (optional)*

If necessary, pound veal slices with a meat mallet to ¼-inch thickness. Ham slices and veal should be about the same size. Place one slice ham on each veal slice. Place 3 orange sections in center of each; roll up and fasten with wooden picks.

In small bowl, beat together egg and milk. Dip each veal roll in egg mixture; coat with mixture of bread crumbs, salt and pepper.

In large skillet, heat oil; sauté veal rolls over moderate heat until lightly browned, 20 to 25 minutes. Drain on paper towels. Place on heated serving dish to keep warm.

Sauté onion in remaining oil until transparent; add ¾ cup orange juice, bring to boiling. Mix together remaining orange juice and cornstarch; blend into onion mixture, bring to a boil. Add dry sherry and orange peel; mix well. Serve sauce over veal rolls.

Garnish platter with orange slices, if desired.

YIELD: 4 to 6 servings.

A robust entrée for a football buffet.

SAVORY BEEF STEW

½	pound bacon, cut into small pieces
¼	cup flour
	Salt and pepper to taste
2½	pounds beef for stew, cut into 2-inch cubes
¼	cup olive oil
3	cups chopped onion
2	large cloves garlic, chopped
1½	cups Florida orange juice
1	cup dry red wine
¾	cup canned tomato purée
2	beef bouillon cubes
1	teaspoon salt
½	teaspoon pepper
¼	teaspoon nutmeg
2	bay leaves
4	medium turnips, cut in chunks (about 4 cups)
5	medium carrots, cut in chunks (about 3 cups)
2	tablespoons chopped parsley

In large kettle or heavy saucepan, sauté bacon until golden brown; remove and drain. Set aside. Combine flour, salt and pepper; dredge beef in flour mixture. Brown meat in bacon fat over high heat; remove meat and reserve.

Add olive oil to pan and heat. Sauté onion and garlic until golden. Add orange juice, wine, tomato purée, bouillon cubes, salt, pepper, nutmeg and bay leaves.

Return bacon and meat to kettle. Cover. Bring to a boil. Reduce heat, simmer 30 minutes.

Add turnips and carrots. Cover. Cook, stirring occasionally, 1 hour longer or until vegetables and meat are tender. Remove bay leaves.

Sprinkle with parsley. Serve with noodles, if desired.

YIELD: 6 to 8 servings.

Photograph, opposite page.

Soused Orange Slices, page 179; Savory Beef Stew

A nourishing, delicious blend of ingredients that has the added advantage of taking very little time to prepare. It also stretches a pound of beef to make dinner for six.

SWEET AND SOUR MEATBALLS

1	*pound ground beef*
¼	*cup packaged dry bread crumbs*
2	*tablespoons water*
1	*egg, lightly beaten*
½	*teaspoon salt*
⅛	*teaspoon pepper*
2	*tablespoons oil*
2¼	*cups Florida grapefruit juice*
1	*can (8 ounces) tomato sauce*
3	*tablespoons brown sugar*
⅓	*cup raisins*

In medium bowl, combine beef, crumbs, water, egg, salt and pepper; mix well. Shape into 12 meatballs.

In large saucepan, heat oil; brown meatballs, a few at a time. Remove meatballs and set aside as they are browned. Pour off excess fat from pan.

Gradually add grapefruit juice to pan, stirring to dissolve bits from bottom of pan. Stir in tomato sauce, sugar and raisins; return meatballs to pan. Cover. Simmer until meat is cooked through, about 10 minutes.

Serve over rice, mashed potatoes or noodles.

YIELD: 4 servings.

FRUITED SHORT RIBS

1	tablespoon vegetable oil
4	pounds short ribs, cut in 2-inch cubes
2½	cups Florida orange juice, divided
1	can (13 ounces) beef broth (1⅔ cups)
¾	teaspoon salt
¾	teaspoon ground cinnamon
¾	teaspoon ground allspice
¼	teaspoon ground cloves
¼	teaspoon pepper
1	package (11 ounces) mixed dried fruit or 1½ cups pitted prunes and dried apricots
2	tablespoons cornstarch
2	Florida oranges, peeled and sectioned

In large kettle or Dutch oven, heat oil; brown meat well on all sides, cooking only a few pieces at a time. Drain off fat.

Add 2¼ cups orange juice, broth, salt, cinnamon, allspice, cloves and pepper. Bring to boiling. Cover. Reduce heat, simmer 1 hour 45 minutes. Skim fat.

Add dried fruit and mix well. Cover, cook 45 minutes longer or until meat is very tender. Skim fat again, if necessary. Combine cornstarch and remaining ¼ cup orange juice; add to stew. Stir until thickened and bubbly.

Just before serving, add orange sections.

YIELD: 6 to 8 servings.

MEXICAN BEEF WITH ORANGE SAUCE

1	4-pound pot roast of beef
	Salt
	Pepper
3	tablespoons vegetable oil
2	celery ribs, diced
2	large onions, diced (2 cups)
1½	cups beef broth
2	cups Florida orange juice
2	cloves garlic, minced
½	teaspoon dried leaf thyme
½	teaspoon ground coriander
¼	teaspoon ground cinnamon
⅛	teaspoon ground cloves
1	Florida orange, thinly sliced

Preheat oven to 350°F.

Sprinkle meat with salt and pepper. Heat oil in Dutch oven or heavy kettle. Brown meat on all sides. Remove from pan. Set aside.

Sauté celery and onions in pan until golden; return meat to pan. Add broth, orange juice, garlic, thyme, coriander, cinnamon and cloves. Cover. Simmer on top of stove, or cook in 350°F. oven 2½ to 3 hours until meat is tender, turning meat occasionally during cooking.

Remove meat from broth, slice into ¼-inch slices; arrange on shallow platter.

Skim fat from broth. Strain broth over meat.

Garnish with orange slices.

YIELD: 6 servings.

This stew freezes beautifully. Freeze extra portions for defrosting and fast preparation whenever time limitations demand a quick dinner.

DIXIE BEEF STEW

1	cup Florida grapefruit juice
1	teaspoon salt
1	clove garlic, minced
1½	pounds beef round, cut in 1-inch cubes
2	tablespoons salad oil
1	large green pepper, chopped
1	large onion, sliced
1	cup chopped fresh tomato
2	tablespoons brown sugar
1	tablespoon red wine vinegar
1	teaspoon dried leaf rosemary
1	bay leaf, crumbled
½	cup sliced, pitted ripe olives

Combine grapefruit juice, salt and garlic in large bowl. Add beef cubes and refrigerate overnight. Drain beef, reserving marinade.

Heat oil in heavy kettle or Dutch oven. Brown beef on all sides; add green pepper and onion and sauté 3 minutes. Add tomato.

Combine reserved marinade with brown sugar, vinegar, rosemary and bay leaf. Add to beef and vegetables. Cover, simmer 45 minutes or until beef is tender. Add olives, simmer 5 minutes longer.

YIELD: 4 servings.

NOTE: To freeze: Freeze stew in freezer bags or containers. To serve, defrost several hours at room temperature or overnight in refrigerator, heat through; do not boil.

Photograph, page 85.

SPICY SKEWERED BEEF

1	cup Florida grapefruit juice
2	tablespoons chopped scallions
2	tablespoons soy sauce
1	clove garlic, minced
2	teaspoons salad oil
2	teaspoons molasses
1	teaspoon ginger
½	teaspoon salt
¾	pound beef round, cut in 1-inch cubes
1	green pepper, cut in 1-inch pieces
1	tomato, cut in 1-inch pieces
1	large onion, cut in 1-inch pieces

Combine first 8 ingredients in medium bowl to make marinade; mix well. Add beef cubes; cover; refrigerate overnight, turning beef once.

Remove beef from marinade and reserve. String beef cubes on skewers, alternating with green pepper, tomato and onion pieces.

Brush beef and vegetables with remaining marinade. Grill or broil 10 to 15 minutes, turning to brown all sides. Baste with remaining marinade during cooking.

Serve with hot cooked rice, if desired.

YIELD: 2 servings.

Photograph, opposite page.

Dixie Beef Stew, page 83; Spicy Skewered Beef

CITRUS LAMB CONNEMARA

Citrus brings a sparkling flavor to an old favorite. Serve with Countryside Cabbage, page 120, for an additional change of pace.

2	tablespoons butter or margarine
½	cup diced onion
1	clove garlic, minced
12	slices raisin bread, crumbled
2	Florida grapefruit, peeled, sectioned (2 cups)
¼	cup coarsely chopped walnuts
1	egg, lightly beaten
½	teaspoon salt
¼	teaspoon dried rosemary, crumbled
2	dashes hot pepper sauce
1	6 to 8 pound leg of lamb, boned and flattened
1	clove garlic, slivered
	Salt and pepper

Preheat oven to 350°F.

In medium skillet, melt butter; sauté onion and minced garlic until soft. Add raisin bread, grapefruit sections, nuts, egg, salt, rosemary and hot pepper sauce.

Spread lean side of meat with stuffing; roll up. Tie meat securely with clean, white string. Make slits in meat in several places with point of sharp knife; insert a sliver of garlic in each slit. Season with salt and pepper.

Place meat on rack in a shallow roasting pan. Roast in a 350°F. oven 2½ to 3 hours until meat thermometer registers 170°F. for medium doneness or 180°F. for well done.

YIELD: 6 to 8 servings.

BAKED FISH BALBOA

2	*tablespoons butter or margarine*
¼	*cup chopped shallots*
½	*cup packaged dried bread crumbs*
⅓	*cup Florida frozen concentrated grapefruit juice, thawed, undiluted, divided*
½	*teaspoon salt, divided*
2	*whole fish, (1½ pounds each), dressed, boned, head on (bluefish, red snapper, sea bass, porgies, sea trout)*
½	*teaspoon dried leaf tarragon*
2	*medium carrots, thinly sliced (1 cup)*
2	*medium ribs celery, julienned (¾ cup)*

Prepare grill so coals are hot when fish is prepared for cooking.

In medium skillet, melt butter; sauté shallots until golden. Remove skillet from heat; stir in bread crumbs, 2 tablespoons grapefruit juice concentrate and ¼ teaspoon salt.

Place each fish on a double thickness of aluminum foil or on heavy duty foil, 6 inches longer than the fish. Spoon bread crumb mixture into the cavity of each fish.

Combine remaining grapefruit juice concentrate, tarragon and remaining ¼ teaspoon salt; brush on both sides of fish. Spoon half the carrots and celery around each fish.

Seal foil tightly by double folding all edges. Place on grill about 6 inches above hot coals. Grill about 30 minutes.

YIELD: 4 servings.

NOTE: To bake fish in the oven: Place foil packets in a shallow baking pan. Bake in a 350°F. oven 40 to 45 minutes, until fish flakes easily when tested with a fork.

Enthusiasm for fish-cookery is one of the noteworthy trends in American cuisine. Fish is lauded as an important food due to its low cholesterol and calorie counts.

SESAME BAKED FISH

2	tablespoons peanut oil
1	clove garlic, minced
1	teaspoon chopped fresh ginger
1	cup sliced celery
1	cup julienned red pepper
3	tablespoons soy sauce
4	teaspoons honey
2	Florida grapefruit, sectioned, juice reserved
1	whole flounder (about 3 pounds), dressed
2	tablespoons sesame seeds

Preheat oven to 425°F.

In medium skillet, heat oil; add garlic and ginger and cook 3 minutes. Add celery and red pepper; stir-fry 1 minute just to coat with seasoned oil. Add soy sauce, honey and juice from grapefruit (about ¼ cup).

Cut diagonal slashes on both sides of fish. Place fish in a shallow baking pan lined with aluminum foil.

Spoon vegetable mixture over fish; sprinkle with sesame seeds.

Bake, uncovered, in a 425°F. oven about 15 minutes or until fish flakes easily with a fork. Halfway through baking period, baste with pan juices; add reserved grapefruit sections.

To serve, spoon vegetables onto a heated serving platter. Lift fish on foil and slide onto serving platter.

YIELD: 4 servings.

NOTE: Red snapper, porgy, or striped bass can be substituted for flounder.

A variety of fish is readily available on today's market. Fish Steaks Veronique is easy to prepare and adaptable to several kinds of fish.

FISH STEAKS VERONIQUE

4	*fish steaks (6 ounces each) or 2 fish steaks (12 ounces each) (halibut, tilefish, salmon)*
3	*tablespoons flour*
¼	*teaspoon salt*
⅛	*teaspoon pepper*
4	*tablespoons butter or margarine, divided*
½	*pound red seedless grapes*
¾	*cup Florida grapefruit juice*
2	*medium Florida grapefruit, sectioned*
2	*tablespoons chopped parsley*

Combine flour, salt and pepper; coat fish steaks with flour mixture. Reserve unused flour mixture.

In large skillet, melt 2 tablespoons butter; sauté steaks until brown on one side, 3 to 4 minutes. Turn and brown other side. Add additional butter while sautéeing if necessary. Fish tests done when it flakes easily with a fork. Remove to serving platter, keep warm.

In same skillet, melt remaining 2 tablespoons butter. Stir in grapes; cook 1 minute. Stir in reserved flour mixture. Gradually add grapefruit juice. Cook, stirring constantly, until mixture boils and thickens.

Add grapefruit sections and parsley; heat through. Pour over fish steaks.

YIELD: 4 servings.

Serve with Asparagus
Maltaise, page 116.

GOLD AND SILVER TREASURE FISH

1	teaspoon cornstarch
1½	tablespoons soy sauce
1½	tablespoons salad oil
1	tablespoon sherry
1	teaspoon sugar
¼	teaspoon salt
¼	teaspoon pepper
3	tablespoons chopped scallions
1	clove garlic, minced
½	teaspoon finely chopped pared ginger root, or ¼ teaspoon ground ginger
3	Florida oranges, peeled and sectioned (1 cup)
1	Florida grapefruit, peeled and sectioned (1 cup)
1	package (6 ounces) frozen snow peas, thawed and drained or ½ pound fresh snow peas
1	pound lean fish, cut in 1-inch cubes (halibut, flounder, tilefish)

Preheat oven to 425° F.

In large bowl, blend cornstarch and soy sauce. Stir in remaining ingredients except for rice. Cover. Marinate in refrigerator 1 hour.

Turn into a 2-quart baking dish; cover. Bake in 425°F. oven 12 to 15 minutes or until fish flakes easily when tested with a fork.

Serve over rice, if desired.

YIELD: 4 servings.

Photograph, opposite page.

A drawn fish is a fish with head, fins and tail remaining. Entrails are removed.

FISH WITH CHINESE CABBAGE

2	tablespoons flour
¾	teaspoon salt, divided
⅛	teaspoon pepper
2	whole fish*, 1½ pounds each, drawn (bluefish, sea bass, whiting, or flounder)
¼	cup olive oil
2	large onions, sliced (2 cups)
2	cloves garlic, minced
1	teaspoon dried leaf oregano, crumbled
¾	cup Florida grapefruit juice
3	tablespoons wine vinegar
8	cups coarsely shredded Chinese cabbage
2	tablespoons diced pimiento
2	medium Florida grapefruit, sectioned

Combine flour, ½ teaspoon salt and pepper. Coat the fish with flour mixture.

In large skillet, heat oil. Pan-fry fish on one side 5 minutes. Turn and fry other side 5 minutes longer or until fish flakes when tested with fork. Remove to serving platter; keep warm.

In same skillet, combine onions, garlic, oregano and remaining ¼ teaspoon salt; cook until vegetables are tender. Stir in grapefruit juice and vinegar; simmer 4 minutes. Add cabbage, stir until limp, 2 to 3 minutes. Stir in pimiento.

Spoon mixture around fish.

Garnish with grapefruit sections.

YIELD: 4 servings.

*NOTE: One large fish weighing 3 to 4 pounds can be used. Place prepared fish on the oiled rack of a broiling pan; baste with olive oil. Broil 10 minutes, 3 to 4 inches from broiling unit. When fish has browned, turn, brush with oil and broil 10 minutes on other side.

Easily transported for picnics. Good with potato salad and cole slaw. Include hard rolls for those preferring a hearty sandwich.

SPICY PORK ROAST

1	smoked pork butt, 2½ to 3 pounds
1	large onion, sliced
1	can (6 ounces) Florida frozen concentrated grapefruit juice, thawed, undiluted
	Water
2	tablespoons catsup
2	tablespoons prepared Dijon-style mustard
2	tablespoons brown sugar
¼	teaspoon ground allspice
	Dash hot pepper sauce
1	Florida grapefruit, peeled, sectioned (optional)

Place pork butt and onion in large saucepan. Add grapefruit juice concentrate and enough water to cover. Bring to a boil. Simmer over medium heat 25 minutes per pound.

Preheat oven to 350° F.

Remove pork to a shallow baking pan. Add ¾ cup of the cooking liquid. In small bowl, combine ¼ cup cooking liquid, catsup, mustard, brown sugar, allspice and pepper sauce. Brush over pork butt.

Roast in a 350° F. oven 30 minutes. Turn meat and brush often with glaze. Remove meat to serving platter. Serve pan liquids with meat.

Garnish with grapefruit sections, if desired.

YIELD: 8 to 10 servings.

Two Florida tangelos, peeled and sectioned, may be used in lieu of grapefruit, if desired.

BRAISED PORK CHOPS WITH GRAPEFRUIT

4	pork chops, cut 1-inch thick
	Flour
2	tablespoons unsalted butter or margarine
1	tablespoon vegetable oil
2	small onions, sliced and separated
2	fresh pears, cored, quartered
½	cup water
1	teaspoon dried leaf marjoram
¼	teaspoon ground cinnamon
2	Florida grapefruit, peeled and sectioned

Flour pork chops liberally on both sides. In large skillet, heat butter and oil over medium heat; brown pork chops on both sides; remove; reserve. Sauté onion rings in fat remaining in skillet. Return chops to skillet; add pears and water; sprinkle with marjoram and cinnamon. Cook over low heat 1 hour and 15 minutes until chops are tender and sauce is thickened. Add grapefruit sections, heat briefly. Serve immediately.

YIELD: 4 servings.

Photograph, page 73.

Hispanic cuisine is identified by its special combinations of herbs and spices, with meats and vegetables and the liberal use of fruit.

PORK ROAST SAN JUAN

8   cloves garlic, divided
1   center cut loin of pork, with backbone cracked (about 4 pounds)
     Peel of 1 Florida orange, cut in pieces
1   tablespoon black peppercorns
1   tablespoon dried leaf oregano
½   teaspoon salt
1¾   cups Florida orange juice, divided
1   tablespoon flour
1   Florida orange, cut in wedges

Preheat oven to 350° F.

Cut 2 cloves of garlic in several pieces. With tip of knife, cut small slits in meat. Insert slivers of garlic in meat.

In container of electric blender, combine remaining 6 cloves garlic, orange peel, peppercorns, oregano, salt and 2 tablespoons orange juice; cover; process to form a paste. Rub paste on meat; wrap with plastic wrap and let stand in refrigerator at least 4 hours or overnight.

Unwrap and place in shallow roasting pan. Roast in a 350° F. oven 30 to 35 minutes per pound. After one hour, baste with orange juice. Baste frequently using about 1½ cups juice.

Remove roast from pan. Cut deep slit between each pork chop. Insert orange wedge into each slit.

To make gravy, combine flour and remaining 2 tablespoons orange juice; pour into roasting pan. Stir over low heat, scraping up bits from bottom of pan, until mixture boils and thickens.

Serve gravy with roast.

YIELD: 4 to 6 servings.

The Chinese were the first to make an art of cooking. Their cuisine still exemplifies how to cook quickly but gently so that the food retains its natural flavor.

CITRUS STIR-FRY

⅓   cup Florida grapefruit juice
3   tablespoons soy sauce
3   tablespoons vegetable oil, divided
½   teaspoon ground ginger
1   pound boneless pork loin, cut into very thin strips
1   tablespoon cornstarch
¾   pound sea scallops, cut into thin slices
1   cup green onions or scallions, cut in 1-inch pieces
2   Florida grapefruit, peeled and sectioned
     Hot, cooked rice
     Green pepper julienned (optional)

In a small bowl, combine grapefruit juice, soy sauce, 1 tablespoon oil and ginger. Add pork strips; cover and let marinate 1 hour at room temperature. Drain pork. Reserve marinade. Combine marinade and cornstarch; set aside.

In a large skillet or wok, heat remaining 2 tablespoons oil over high heat. Add pork and stir-fry 2 to 3 minutes until browned. Add scallops and continue stir-frying another 2 minutes. Add reserved marinade mixture and green onions, continue stirring until sauce boils and thickens. Gently stir in grapefruit sections. Serve over hot rice.

Garnish with green pepper, if desired.

YIELD: 6 servings.

ORANGE SPARERIBS SARASOTA

4 to 5	pounds spareribs, cut in serving pieces
1	can (6 ounces) Florida frozen concentrated orange juice, thawed, undiluted
¾	cup catsup
2	tablespoons molasses
1	teaspoon Worcestershire sauce
½	teaspoon hot pepper sauce
1	teaspoon salt
4	teaspoons grated onion
1	orange, sliced

Place spareribs in large kettle; cover with water and bring to a boil. Reduce heat and simmer, covered, for 30 minutes. Drain and refrigerate until ready to grill.

Mix undiluted orange juice concentrate with remaining ingredients.

Place spareribs on grill set 6 to 8 inches from heat. Cook 15 minutes; turn and brush with orange sauce. Cook 15 to 30 minutes longer, turning and brushing frequently with sauce.

Garnish with orange slices.

YIELD: 4 to 6 servings.

SALMON CREPES

1	recipe crepes
¼	cup butter or margarine
1	cup chopped onions
¼	cup flour
1	cup Florida grapefruit juice
1	cup chicken broth
1	teaspoon Worcestershire sauce
1	teaspoon salt
¾	teaspoon dried dill weed
1	bay leaf
2 or 3	dashes hot pepper sauce
1	can (1 pound) pink salmon, drained, boned, broken in chunks
1½	cups diced cooked potatoes (2 medium)
1	Florida grapefruit, peeled, sectioned
1	tablespoon chopped parsley

Prepare one recipe crepes*; set aside.

In medium saucepan, melt butter over medium heat; sauté onions until golden. Stir in flour, cook 1 minute. Gradually stir in grapefruit juice and chicken broth; add Worcestershire sauce, salt, dill weed, bay leaf and hot pepper sauce. Cook, stirring constantly, until sauce thickens and boils, cook 2 minutes longer.

In medium bowl, combine salmon, potatoes, and 1 cup of the grapefruit sauce; mix gently.

Place 2 heaping tablespoons salmon filling on each crepe; roll crepes; place side by side in a 12-inch skillet. Pour remaining grapefruit sauce over crepes. Cover skillet. Heat slowly 10 minutes.

Just before serving, add grapefruit sections and sprinkle with parsley.

YIELD: 4 to 6 servings.

Photograph, opposite page.

continued

Salmon Crepes; Orange-Cheese Blintzes, page 102; Cannelloni a la Lombardi, page 104

*CREPES

4	eggs
½	cup milk
⅛	teaspoon salt
6	tablespoons whole wheat flour
	Butter for frying

In small bowl of electric mixer, combine eggs, milk, salt and flour. Beat until smooth.

Cook crepes in hot, buttered, 6-inch skillet, using about 2 tablespoons of batter for each crepe. Tilt pan quickly to make a very thin crepe. Brown lightly on one side, turn to brown other side. Repeat with remaining batter.

If making crepes ahead, wrap loosely in foil or place in airtight container and refrigerate until ready to use.

YIELD: 12 crepes.

A traditional Swiss recipe.

FLORIDA MUESLI

3	cups wheat flakes
2	cups bran flakes
1	cup regular oats, uncooked
1	cup coarsely chopped nuts
½	cup raisins
½	cup brown sugar, well crumbled
1	cup plain yogurt
4	cups Florida orange and grapefruit sections

Mix cereals, raisins, nuts and brown sugar; place in container with tight-fitting cover.

At serving time, mix with yogurt, orange and grapefruit sections.

YIELD: 6 servings.

Bulgar wheat is a staple of Middle East cooking.

ORANGE-BULGAR VEGETARIAN CASSEROLE

¼	cup unsalted butter or margarine
½	cup chopped onion
½	cup chopped celery
1	clove garlic, minced
1	cup uncooked bulgar wheat
1	cup Florida orange juice
1	cup water
1	can (15 ounces) kidney beans, drained
¼	pound fresh mushrooms, sliced
⅓	cup raisins
¼	cup wheat germ
2	Florida oranges, peeled and sectioned

In large skillet, melt butter over medium heat; sauté onion, celery and garlic 1 minute. Add bulgar, continue to cook, stirring 5 minutes.

Stir in orange juice and water, bring to a boil. Add kidney beans, mushrooms, raisins and wheat germ. Reduce heat and simmer, covered 15 to 20 minutes until bulgar is tender and all liquid is absorbed. Spoon into serving dish.

Garnish with orange sections.

YIELD: 4 to 6 servings.

Photograph, page 73.

NOTE: This mixture is excellent used as a stuffing for whole vegetables. Fill tomatoes, Bell peppers or squash halves with cooked bulgar mixture. Bake in moderate oven until vegetable is tender.

Crepes may be prepared up to one month in advance and kept frozen for use as needed. Stack cooked crepes in layers, separated by wax paper. Secure the package in well-sealed freezer wrap. To use, allow crepes to thaw completely at room temperature.

ORANGE-CHEESE BLINTZES

1	recipe Orange Crepes
1	cup (8-ounce carton) cream style cottage cheese
1	package (3 ounces) cream cheese, softened at room temperature
1	tablespoon sugar
1	egg yolk, lightly beaten
1	Florida orange, peeled, sectioned, cut in pieces
¼	teaspoon salt
⅛	teaspoon cinnamon
	Butter or margarine
	Orange sections

Prepare 1 recipe Orange Crepes*; set aside.

In small bowl, combine cottage cheese, cream cheese, sugar, egg yolk, orange, salt and cinnamon; mix well.

Place 2 heaping tablespoons cheese filling in center of browned side of each crepe. Fold over from both sides, then from top and bottom to form a small envelope. Repeat until all crepes and filling have been used.

Melt butter in skillet, brown blintzes on both sides.

To serve, arrange blintzes on serving dish, pour Orange Sauce** in center and garnish with orange sections.

YIELD: 12 blintzes.

continued

ORANGE CREPES

2	*eggs, beaten*
½	*cup Florida orange juice*
⅓	*cup water*
¾	*cup flour*
1	*tablespoon oil*
1	*teaspoon sugar*
½	*teaspoon grated orange peel*
¼	*teaspoon salt*

In small bowl, beat eggs, orange juice, water, flour, oil, sugar, orange peel and salt until batter is smooth.

Cook on hot, greased, 6-inch skillet, using about 2 tablespoons batter for each crepe. Tilt pan quickly to spread batter evenly. Brown on one side only; stack, browned side up, between pieces of waxed paper. Repeat until all batter is used.

YIELD: 12 crepes.

**ORANGE SAUCE*

3	*tablespoons sugar*
1	*tablespoon cornstarch*
⅛	*teaspoon salt*
⅔	*cup Florida orange juice*
⅓	*cup sour cream*
2	*Florida oranges, peeled, sectioned*

In small saucepan, combine sugar, cornstarch and salt. Gradually stir in orange juice; cook, stirring constantly, until mixture thickens and comes to boiling.

Cool slightly. Stir in sour cream. Just before serving, gently fold in orange sections.

YIELD: 1¼ cups.

Photograph, page 99.

Cannelloni is a pasta meant for stuffing. Translated into English, it means "big pipes," so you can imagine how plumply it may be filled.

CANNELLONI A LA LOMBARDI

1   recipe Cannelloni crepes
2   pounds fresh spinach, cooked, chopped, drained
2   tablespoons olive oil
1   large or 2 small cloves garlic, sliced
6   eggs
3   tablespoons milk
½   teaspoon salt
2   tablespoons butter or margarine
¼   cup grated Parmesan cheese

Prepare one recipe Cannelloni Crepes*, set aside.

Put spinach in a sieve or colander; press with back of spoon to remove excess moisture. In large skillet, heat oil; sauté garlic until light brown, remove garlic from skillet. Add spinach to skillet; stir until heated through. Remove spinach and reserve.

In medium bowl, beat eggs with milk and salt. In same skillet, melt butter over low heat; pour in eggs; cook, stirring constantly, until eggs are thickened but still moist.

Preheat oven to 350°F.

To assemble crepes, place 2 heaping tablespoons of spinach on each crepe. Top with 2 tablespoons cooked egg. Sprinkle lightly with Parmesan cheese. Roll crepes. Place side by side in a buttered 9 x 13 x 2-inch baking dish. Pour Fresh Tomato Sauce** over all. Bake in a 350°F. oven 10 minutes or until heated through.

YIELD: About 6 to 8 servings.

*CANNELLONI CREPES

4   eggs
½   cup Florida orange juice
½   teaspoon grated orange peel
⅛   teaspoon salt
6   tablespoons flour
     Butter for frying

continued

In small bowl of electric mixer, beat together eggs, orange juice, orange peel and salt. Gradually add flour, beating until batter is smooth.

Cook in hot, buttered, 6-inch skillet, using 2 tablespoons batter for each crepe, tilting pan quickly to make a very thin crepe. Cook 1 to 2 minutes on each side, or until delicately brown. Repeat with remaining batter. Add butter as necessary.

Crepes may be made ahead and wrapped loosely in aluminum foil or place in airtight container and refrigerate until ready to use.

YIELD: 14 to 16 crepes.

**FRESH TOMATO SAUCE

2	*large fresh tomatoes*
¼	*cup butter or margarine*
1	*large or 2 small cloves garlic, sliced*
½	*cup Florida orange juice*
½	*teaspoon salt*
¼	*teaspoon dried leaf basil, crumbled*
1	*can (2½ ounces) sliced mushrooms, drained*
2	*Florida oranges, peeled, sectioned*

Peel tomatoes, cut in half. Gently squeeze to remove seeds and excess moisture. Dice.

In medium saucepan, melt butter; sauté garlic until light brown, remove garlic. Add diced tomatoes, orange juice, salt and basil. Cover. Cook over low heat 15 minutes, stirring occasionally.

Add mushrooms and orange sections; mix gently. Spoon over cannelloni.

YIELD: 1½ to 2 cups.

NOTE: To make peeling tomatoes easier, drop in scalding hot water for one or two minutes.

Photograph, page 99.

When making two omelets for eight servings, use two skillets.

PUFFY OMELET WITH ORANGE SAUCE

6   *large eggs, separated*
⅓   *cup Florida orange juice*
¼   *teaspoon cream of tartar*
      Pinch of salt (optional)
2   *tablespoons vegetable oil*
2   *tablespoons butter or margarine*
      Sour cream (optional)

Preheat oven to 350°F.

In small mixing bowl, beat egg yolks until thick. Gradually add orange juice while beating.

In large mixing bowl, beat egg whites with cream of tartar and salt until stiff, but not dry. Fold yolk mixture into whites.

In a 10-inch skillet with an oven-proof handle, heat oil and butter together. Pour in egg mixture. Cook over medium heat until bottom is golden.

Place skillet in a 350°F. oven. Bake 15 to 20 minutes until eggs puff and mixture is firm. Remove from oven. Make a 1-inch deep cut across omelet, slightly off center. Fold smaller part over larger part. Turn out onto platter.

Spoon Orange Sauce* over top. Serve with sour cream, if desired.

YIELD: 4 servings.

continued

*ORANGE SAUCE

3 *tablespoons brown sugar*
2 *tablespoons cornstarch*
1 *teaspoon ground cardamom*
1½ *cups Florida orange juice*
½ *teaspoon vanilla*
3 *Florida oranges, peeled and sectioned*

In medium saucepan, combine sugar, cornstarch and cardamom. Gradually add orange juice. Heat, stirring constantly, until mixture boils and thickens. Stir in vanilla and orange sections.

YIELD: About 3 cups.

Vegetables
and
Accompaniments

Vegetables and Accompaniments

The increased interest in regional, continental and ethnic cooking has provided a real bonanza for vegetables and accompaniments. With some citrus pizzazz, these wondrously-varied, delicious and nutritious foods shimmer with new-found charisma.

See for yourself what a flourish of oranges, grapefruit, tangerines and tangelos can do for broccoli, green beans, asparagus, onions, potatoes and other vegetables. Citrus can perk up any fruit, gelatine or sauce. Relishes go contemporary with a boost from citrus pieces, peel and juices.

Citrus adds marvelous new textures and splashes of eye-catching color to vegetables and accompaniments. Contrasting the bright hues of vegetables with the golds and oranges of Florida citrus will make your dishes look and taste more appealing.

Vegetables and accompaniments are increasingly important to today's good-sense-with-good-taste eating. Welcome to an array of revitalizing recipes a la citrus!

Provolone cheese is an Italian
cheese that is gaining
popularity because of the
pleasing flavor it adds to many
recipes.

BROCCOLI GRAPEFRUIT CASSEROLE

1	large bunch fresh broccoli, trimmed
2	Florida grapefruit peeled and sectioned
1	cup (4 ounces) grated Provolone cheese
½	cup sliced, pitted, black olives
⅛	teaspoon salt
⅛	teaspoon pepper

Cook broccoli in 1-inch boiling salted water until crisp-tender; drain. Arrange broccoli and grapefruit sections in buttered, 1½-quart, heat-proof casserole. Sprinkle with cheese, olives, salt, and pepper. Place under preheated broiler until cheese is melted and grapefruit sections are heated through.

YIELD: 4 to 6 servings.

BROCCOLI AND ROMAINE WITH GRAPEFRUIT

1	large or 2 small bunches fresh broccoli
1	head romaine
2	tablespoons sesame seeds
⅓	cup vegetable oil
½	teaspoon salt
2	Florida grapefruit, peeled and sectioned

Cut broccoli spears in half lengthwise; cut any long spears in half crosswise. Wash romaine leaves; break into bite-size pieces. Brown sesame seeds in large skillet or wok over medium heat; remove to bowl; reserve.

Heat oil in same skillet. Add broccoli. Cook, stirring quickly and often, until crisp-tender. Add romaine and salt. Cook, stirring constantly, 2 minutes. Remove from heat. Stir in sesame seeds and grapefruit sections.

YIELD: 8 servings.

A medley of vegetables steamed lightly so that each vegetable retains its fresh flavor and texture. Orange juice and honey add healthy natural sweetness to this traditional Jewish dish.

TZIMMES

2	pounds carrots, pared, thinly sliced
1	medium onion, chopped
24	pitted prunes
¼	cup butter or margarine
½	cup firmly packed light brown sugar
½	teaspoon salt
¼	teaspoon ground cinnamon
⅛	teaspoon ground nutmeg
1	cup Florida orange juice

In large saucepan, combine carrots and onion. Add water just to cover, bring to a boil over high heat. Boil rapidly 25 minutes or until carrots are very tender. Drain.

Preheat oven to 350°F.

Place carrots evenly in a 2-quart shallow baking dish. Add prunes. In small saucepan, melt butter; add brown sugar, salt, cinnamon and nutmeg, stir until smooth. Add orange juice; pour over casserole. Bake in a 350°F. oven 1 hour, 20 minutes. Stir every 20 minutes during baking.

Serve in same dish.

YIELD: 8 servings.

A good buffet vegetable.

HARVEST MEDLEY

2	*medium zucchini sliced ¼-inch thick (1½ cups)*
2	*medium carrots, cut in julienne strips (1½ cups)*
1	*medium rutabaga, peeled, cubed (1½ cups)*
1	*large onion, diced (1 cup)*
¾	*cup chicken broth*
6	*tablespoons (½ of 6-ounce can) Florida frozen concentrated orange juice, thawed, undiluted*
½	*teaspoon salt*
¼	*teaspoon ground nutmeg*
3	*tablespoons butter or margarine*
1½	*cups fresh whole wheat bread or corn bread crumbs*
½	*cup chopped nuts*

Preheat oven to 350°F.

In 2-quart shallow casserole, combine zucchini, carrots, rutabaga, onion, broth, orange juice concentrate, salt and nutmeg; mix well.

In medium skillet, melt butter; add crumbs and nuts; toss until well coated. Sprinkle crumbs over vegetables.

Bake in a 350°F. oven 1 hour or until vegetables are tender.

YIELD: 6 servings.

A healthy meal or side dish for people on the go.

CHINESE VEGETABLES A LA FLORIDA

2	cups carrots, cut in 2-inch pieces
2	cups celery, cut in 2-inch pieces
1	cup broccoli stems, cut in 2-inch pieces
1	cup fresh green beans, cut in 2-inch pieces
1	large onion, sliced
½	teaspoon salt
1¾	cups Florida grapefruit juice, divided
1	cup broccoli flowerets
4	teaspoons cornstarch
	Soy sauce (optional)

In large saucepan, combine carrots, celery, broccoli stems, green beans, onion, salt and 1 cup grapefruit juice; bring to a boil. Cover; simmer 8 minutes. Add broccoli flowerets. Cover. Cook 5 minutes or until vegetables are crisp-tender.

Blend cornstarch with remaining ¾ cup grapefruit juice; pour over vegetables; bring to a boil, stirring constantly, until thickened. Serve at once with soy sauce, if desired.

YIELD: 4 servings.

A crisp-tender texture and delicate flavor make this dish a marvelous accompaniment to a fish dinner.

CUCUMBERS FLORIDA

3	tablespoons butter or margarine
6	medium-size cucumbers, peeled and sliced
1	teaspoon dried leaf thyme, crumbled
1	teaspoon salt
¼	teaspoon pepper
2	tablespoons cornstarch
1½	cups Florida orange juice

In large skillet, melt butter; sauté cucumbers 3 minutes. Add thyme, salt and pepper; blend well. Dissolve cornstarch in orange juice. Stir into skillet; blend well. Cook, stirring constantly, until mixture boils and thickens.

YIELD: 8 servings.

Like other recipes in this cookbook, parsley is called for here. Fresh parsley is especially good and may be wrapped in baggies and frozen for use as needed.

GREEN BEANS WITH GRAPEFRUIT

1	pound fresh green beans
2	tablespoons butter or margarine
¼	cup minced onion
1	clove garlic, minced
2	tablespoons chopped parsley
¼	teaspoon dried leaf rosemary, crumbled
¼	teaspoon dried leaf basil, crumbled
¼	teaspoon salt
1	Florida grapefruit, peeled and sectioned

Wash beans; remove ends and string, if any. Cut into 2-inch pieces. Cook in ½-inch boiling, salted water (⅛ teaspoon salt per 1 cup water), covered, about 15 minutes or until just tender. Drain.

Melt butter in saucepan. Add onion and garlic; sauté 5 minutes. Add parsley, rosemary, basil and salt. Simmer, covered, 10 minutes. Remove cover, add grapefruit sections; heat through.

To serve, turn beans into serving dish; arrange grapefruit mixture over top.

YIELD: 4 servings.

When trimming asparagus ends at the bottom of each stalk, trim at point where knife goes through easiest. This will cut off any part of the stalk that is not tender.

ASPARAGUS MALTAISE

6   egg yolks
¼   cup Florida frozen concentrated orange juice, thawed, undiluted
¼   teaspoon salt
     Dash hot pepper sauce
1   cup butter or margarine, melted
⅓   cup boiling water
2   pounds asparagus, cooked

In container of electric blender, combine egg yolks, orange juice concentrate, salt and hot pepper sauce. Cover. Process 30 seconds. While blender is still running, remove cover and gradually add melted butter and boiling water. Spoon over cooked asparagus.

To keep sauce hot or to reheat, pour sauce in small bowl, set bowl in pan of hot water until warm.

YIELD: 1½ cups sauce (6 servings).

NEW POTATOES A LA FLORIDA

2   pounds small new potatoes
1   can (6 ounces) Florida frozen concentrated grapefruit juice, thawed, divided
½   teaspoon salt
½   cup butter or margarine, melted
¼   cup minced chives

Scrub potatoes; peel a strip 1-inch wide around middle of each.

In large saucepan, combine potatoes, 6 tablespoons grapefruit juice concentrate, salt and enough water to cover potatoes. Bring to boiling. Cover; simmer 30 to 35 minutes or until potatoes are tender. Drain.

In medium bowl, combine butter and remaining grapefruit juice concentrate; add potatoes and toss gently. Sprinkle with chives.

YIELD: 6 to 8 servings.

GLAZED SWEET POTATOES AND TURNIPS

4	*medium-size sweet potatoes, peeled, cut in chunks*
4	*medium-size turnips, peeled, cut in chunks*
1	*cup Florida orange juice*
⅓	*cup brown sugar*
¼	*cup butter or margarine, melted*
½	*teaspoon mace*
½	*teaspoon salt*
2	*Florida oranges, peeled, sliced*

In a large saucepan in 1-inch boiling water, cook potatoes and turnips until tender but still firm, about 30 minutes.

Preheat oven to 400°F.

Place vegetables in a 2-quart shallow baking dish. In small bowl, combine orange juice, sugar, butter, mace and salt. Pour over vegetables.

Bake, uncovered, in a 400°F. oven about 30 minutes. Baste often with pan juices. Vegetables are done when pan juices are reduced and vegetables are glazed.

Garnish with orange slices.

YIELD: 8 servings.

PIQUANT ONIONS

3	*pounds small, whole white onions*
¼	*cup butter or margarine*
¾	*cup beef broth (not condensed)*
¾	*cup Florida orange juice*
1	*can (8 ounces each) tomato sauce*
2	*tablespoons cider vinegar*
½	*cup seedless dark raisins*
1	*tablespoon sugar*
¼	*teaspoon dried leaf thyme, crumbled*
½	*teaspoon salt*
1	*bay leaf*

Peel onions. Cut an "X" in stem ends to prevent onions from splitting. In large skillet, melt butter; sauté onions until lightly browned.

Add beef broth, orange juice, tomato sauce, vinegar, raisins, sugar, thyme, salt and bay leaf. Bring to a boil; reduce heat, simmer 40 to 45 minutes, uncovered, or until onions are tender. Remove bay leaf.

YIELD: 8 to 10 servings.

Photograph, opposite page.

Orange-Chestnut Stuffed Turkey, page 69; Orange Pumpkin Cake, page 176; Piquant Onions; Spiced Oranges and Pears, page 123

GLAZED BRUSSELS SPROUTS WITH TANGERINES

2	*Florida tangerines*
½	*cup butter or margarine*
½	*cup light brown sugar*
1	*cup Florida tangerine juice*
¼	*teaspoon salt*
2	*pints fresh brussels sprouts, cooked until tender and drained*

Peel tangerines, remove white membrane. Pull sections apart, cut off center section membrane with scissors. Remove seeds. Reserve tangerine sections.

In large skillet, melt butter. Add brown sugar and tangerine juice. Simmer 15 minutes. Add salt and cooked brussels sprouts. Cook over medium heat until sprouts are thoroughly heated and glazed. Add tangerine sections, stir. Serve immediately.

YIELD: 6 servings.

COUNTRYSIDE CABBAGE

2	*tablespoons butter or margarine*
1	*cup sliced onion*
6	*cups shredded red cabbage*
1	*apple, cored, pared and shredded*
1	*cup Florida orange juice*
½	*teaspoon salt*
1	*bay leaf*
2	*Florida oranges, peeled, sectioned (1 cup)*

In large kettle or Dutch oven melt butter; sauté onion until soft. Add cabbage, apple, orange juice, salt and bay leaf; mix well.

Cover; simmer, stirring occasionally, 1½ hours until liquid is absorbed and cabbage is tender.

Just before serving, stir in orange sections.

YIELD: 6 servings.

During the winter months, three tangelos, substituted for oranges, are recommended for a unique taste.

CHINESE CABBAGE AND CELERY WITH ORANGES

2	*tablespoons vegetable oil*
1½	*teaspoons chopped fresh ginger*
5	*ribs celery, sliced in ½-inch pieces (3 cups)*
1	*medium onion, sliced (¾ cup)*
1	*medium head Chinese cabbage, sliced in ½-inch pieces (8 cups)*
1	*can (8 ounces) water chestnuts, drained, sliced*
2	*tablespoons soy sauce*
	Pinch pepper
3	*Florida oranges, peeled and sectioned*
2	*tablespoons sesame seeds, toasted**

In large skillet, heat oil; sauté ginger until golden. Add celery and onion; stir until crisp-tender, about 3 minutes. Add cabbage, water chestnuts, soy sauce and pepper. Stir-fry until cabbage is crisp-tender, about 3 minutes. Gently stir in orange sections.

Spoon mixture into serving bowl; sprinkle with toasted sesame seeds. Serve immediately.

YIELD: 4 to 6 servings.

****NOTE:** To toast sesame seeds, place seeds on shallow baking pan in 350°F. oven for 7 to 10 minutes, stirring frequently.

ORANGE ALMOND RICE

6	tablespoons butter or margarine
2	cups Florida orange juice
1	cup water
2	teaspoons salt
1½	cups raw, long-grain rice
½	cup sliced, blanched almonds
⅓	cup chopped parsley

Combine butter, orange juice, water, salt and rice in 3-quart saucepan. Bring to boiling, stirring once or twice. Reduce heat; cover. Cook, without removing cover or stirring, 15 to 20 minutes or until liquid is absorbed and rice is tender.

Meanwhile, place almonds in small skillet. Toast, over medium heat, stirring constantly, until golden brown. Stir almonds and parsley into rice.

YIELD: 8 servings.
Photograph, page 67.

Colonial wives often kept a pot of baked beans simmering gently on the back of the stove. This dish is perhaps the most universally popular of the great rib-sticking dishes contrived by early New Englanders.

REVOLUTIONARY BAKED BEANS

1	pound dry white beans
2	cups Florida orange juice
1	can (8 ounces) tomato sauce
¾	cup chopped onion
¼	cup molasses
2	tablespoons Worcestershire sauce
¼	pound salt pork, cut in ¾-inch cubes

Soak beans overnight or according to package directions. Bring beans to boiling; simmer 30 minutes. Drain; reserve liquid, adding water if necessary to measure 2 cups. Transfer beans to a 3-quart casserole or bean pot.

Preheat oven to 300°F.

Add 2 cups bean liquid, orange juice, tomato sauce, onion, molasses, Worcestershire and salt pork; mix well. Cover. Bake in a 300°F. oven 4 to 5 hours; stir at least once every hour. Bake uncovered during last hour to thicken sauce.

YIELD: 8 to 10 servings.

Molded Grapefruit Slaw will take center stage on any table with its ruby red appearance provided by red cabbage.

MOLDED GRAPEFRUIT SLAW

2	envelopes unflavored gelatine
1	tablespoon sugar
1	teaspoon salt
1	cup water
2	cups Florida grapefruit juice
¼	cup cider vinegar
1½	cups shredded red cabbage
1	cup finely sliced celery
¼	green pepper, chopped

In medium saucepan, combine gelatine, sugar and salt. Stir in water; let stand 1 minute. Cook over low heat, stirring constantly, until gelatine is dissolved. Stir in grapefruit juice and vinegar. Chill until mixture is consistency of unbeaten egg white. Stir in cabbage, celery and green pepper. Spoon into a 1-quart mold. Chill until firm.

YIELD: 10 servings.

NOTE: Recipe may be doubled to fit an 8-cup mold (as pictured).

Photograph, page 127.

This relish may be prepared in advance and it adds a special color to your presentation. A tasty relish that goes well with poultry, veal and pork.

SPICED ORANGES AND PEARS

3	Florida oranges	2	cinnamon sticks,
1¼	cups sugar	1	tablespoon thinly sliced
1	cup water		fresh ginger
⅔	cup cider vinegar	1	large firm pear, cored
10	whole cloves		and thinly sliced
			(unpared)

Place whole, unpeeled oranges in medium saucepan; cover with water; bring to a boil. Boil 20 minutes or until skins are easily pierced with a fork. Drain. Cut each orange into 8 wedges.

In same saucepan, combine sugar, water, vinegar, cloves, cinnamon and ginger; stir over low heat until sugar dissolves. Bring to a boil; add orange wedges, reduce heat, simmer 15 minutes. Add pear slices; cook 5 to 8 minutes or until tender. Cool. Cover. Chill. Relish will last several weeks if stored in a covered container in the refrigerator.

YIELD: About 1 quart.

Photograph, page 119.

123

Marinades expand the enjoyment of food, tenderizing meat and adding complex flavor. Almost all poultry, meat and game can be marinated. This sauce can be refrigerated for several weeks in a tightly closed jar.

ALL-PURPOSE CITRUS MARINADE

1½   cups Florida grapefruit juice
½   cup olive oil
⅓   cup tomato paste
2   teaspoons salt
1   teaspoon dried leaf oregano, crumbled
1   teaspoon dried leaf thyme, crumbled
1   teaspoon dried leaf basil, crumbled
1   clove garlic, crushed

In bowl or jar, combine all ingredients; blend well. Use to marinate lamb, beef or chicken. Grill or cook as desired. Any leftover marinade may be heated and served as an accompaniment.

YIELD: About 2½ cups, enough to marinate 4 to 5 pounds of meat.

NOTE: A rule of thumb is to marinate at room temperature 1 hour, or 2 or 3 hours in the refrigerator. Marinate overnight in refrigerator if a stronger flavor is desired.

The delicacy of ginger and citrus makes this marinade ideal for chicken and fish, while the assertiveness of garlic and scallions perfectly complement beef, duck and pork.

GRAPEFRUIT MARINADE ORIENTAL

1   cup Florida grapefruit juice
¼   cup vegetable oil
1   tablespoon honey
¼   teaspoon ground ginger
1   small clove garlic, minced
2   scallions, chopped

In bowl or jar, combine grapefruit juice, oil, honey, ginger, garlic and scallions; mix well. Cover. Let stand at room temperature 2 to 3 hours before using.

Use to marinate chicken, duck, fish, or pork. Marinate 1 to 2 hours. Broil meat until tender, basting meat often with marinade as it cooks.

YIELD: 1¼ cups marinade, enough for 2 to 3 pounds of meat.

GRAPEFRUIT SAUCE

1	*cup Florida grapefruit juice*
1	*cup chicken broth*
1	*carrot, cut in 2-inch pieces*
1	*medium onion, quartered*
1	*teaspoon ground cumin*
½	*teaspoon salt*
¼	*teaspoon pepper*
1	*tablespoon butter or margarine*
1	*tablespoon flour*
1	*Florida grapefruit, peeled, sectioned, drained*
2	*tablespoons chopped parsley*

In medium saucepan, combine grapefruit juice, broth, carrot, onion, cumin, salt and pepper. Cook over high heat until liquid is reduced to 1 cup and vegetables are tender (about 15 minutes). Remove vegetables; discard onion and cut carrots into julienne pieces.

Blend butter and flour together; stir into liquid in saucepan. Cook until sauce boils and thickens. Add grapefruit sections, julienne carrot and parsley. Serve over fish, chicken, veal or croquettes.

YIELD: About 1½ cups sauce.

SUNSHINE BARBECUE SAUCE

1	*cup catsup*
1	*can (6 ounces) Florida frozen concentrated orange juice, thawed, undiluted*
¼	*cup cider vinegar*
1	*tablespoon prepared horseradish*
¼	*teaspoon hot pepper sauce*
¼	*teaspoon garlic powder*

In small saucepan, combine all ingredients; bring to boiling. Reduce heat, simmer 15 minutes; cool. Cover, chill. Use as barbecue basting sauce with spareribs, chicken, duck, pork chops, hamburgers, meatloaf or frankfurters.

YIELD: 2 cups.

Try this relish as a vegetable.

FLORIDA FRUIT RELISH

7	medium-size ripe tomatoes, cubed
3	medium pears, pared, cored, cubed
3	medium onions, cubed
3	medium green peppers, cubed
1	Florida orange, unpeeled, sliced ¼-inch thick, cut into small wedges
1½	cups cider vinegar
1	cup Florida orange juice
½	cup sugar
2	tablespoons pickling spice, tied in cheesecloth
1	tablespoon salt

In a large saucepan or kettle, combine all ingredients. Cook over low heat, uncovered, 2 hours. Stir frequently to prevent mixture from sticking to pan.

Relish is ready when it is about the thickness of applesauce. Pour into jars. Cover. Refrigerate up to 6 weeks.

YIELD: 6 cups.

Photograph, opposite page.

HOMESTEAD CORN RELISH

4	cups cooked or canned corn niblets, drained
1	red pepper, chopped
1	green pepper, chopped
½	cup chopped onion
½	cup chopped celery
1	cup Florida orange juice
1	cup cider vinegar
¼	cup sugar
2	teaspoons mustard seed
1½	teaspoons salt

In large saucepan, combine all ingredients. Cook uncovered, 15 to 20 minutes, stirring occasionally. Store in jars in refrigerator up to 6 weeks.

YIELD: 6 cups.

Photograph, opposite page.

Molded Grapefruit Slaw, top, page 123; Florida Fruit Relish, middle; Homestead Corn Relish, bottom

This recipe will work with orange and lime peels, too. The yellow, orange and green peels make a pretty combination in a gift jar.

CANDIED GRAPEFRUIT PEEL

2   Florida grapefruit
1   cup sugar
½   cup light corn syrup
1   cup water
       Granulated sugar

Remove peel from grapefruit in strips with vegetable peeler. Place peel in a medium saucepan, cover with cold water; boil 5 minutes; drain. Repeat 3 times. Dry well on paper towels. Cut peel with knife or scissors into strips ¼-inch in width.

Combine sugar, corn syrup and water in saucepan. Stir over low heat until sugar dissolves. Add grapefruit peel and bring to a boil. Cook over low heat about 40 minutes, until most of the syrup is absorbed. Drain off excess syrup.

Roll peel, a few pieces at a time, in granulated sugar. Place on wire rack and let dry for 24 hours. When dry, store in covered container.

YIELD: Approximately 1 cup.

SAVORY GRAPEFRUIT JELLY

1⅓   cups boiling water
¼   cup dried leaf savory, crumbled
2   large Florida grapefruit, peeled and sectioned
          (reserve juice)
5   cups sugar
2   bottles (6 ounces each) liquid pectin

In a small bowl, combine water and savory. Cover. Let stand 15 minutes; strain into a large saucepan. Add grapefruit sections, any juice reserved from sectioning and sugar. Heat to boiling, stirring to dissolve sugar. Add pectin, stirring constantly. Boil rapidly 1 minute. Pour into hot, sterilized jars. Seal. Or, jelly can be stored in refrigerator, unsealed, up to 6 weeks.

YIELD: Seven ½ pints.

Excellent with your favorite bread at any meal.

FLORIDA ORANGE MARMALADE

6	large Florida oranges
	Water
	Sugar
2	tablespoons lemon juice
	Paraffin

Wash oranges thoroughly, cut in half lengthwise. Remove core and seeds; slice oranges thinly. Measure before placing in large pot and combine with 2 cups of water for each cup of fruit. Bring to a boil. Cover, and let stand overnight.

Bring orange mixture to a boil again, reduce heat and simmer until tender, about 30 minutes. Add ¾ cup sugar for each cup of orange mixture; add lemon juice.

Cook, stirring to dissolve sugar. Boil, uncovered, until of desired consistency, about 2 hours. Stir often to prevent sticking.

Skim off foam with a metal spoon. Ladle marmalade into hot sterilized jars and seal with paraffin.

YIELD: About 8 cups.

NOTE: Melt paraffin over very low heat or over hot water. (If paraffin becomes very hot, it pulls away from jar). Let the marmalade cool to point of setting before covering with coating of melted paraffin approximately ⅛-inch thick. When pouring paraffin, pour from pitcher or spouted pan so marmalade is covered with very thin coating.

An excellent, prepare-in-advance appetizer.

GRAPEFRUIT AND SHRIMP MOUSSE

6	small Florida grapefruit
1	envelope unflavored gelatine
½	cup water
½	cup mayonnaise
½	cup chili sauce
½	teaspoon prepared horseradish
¼	teaspoon salt
½	cup heavy cream, whipped
1	cup cooked shrimp, diced
½	cup chopped celery
6	Florida grapefruit sections (optional)
6	whole shrimp (optional)
	Lettuce

Slice tops off grapefruit. Using a sharp knife, cut a scalloped edge around each grapefruit. Loosen sections from membrane and reserve. Scoop out membrane from shells and discard. Set grapefruit aside.

Combine gelatine and water in medium saucepan. Stir over low heat until gelatine is dissolved. Remove from heat. Add mayonnaise, chili sauce, horseradish and salt. Chill until consistency of unbeaten egg white.

Fold in whipped cream. Fold in 1 cup reserved grapefruit sections, shrimp and celery. Turn into prepared grapefruit shells. Chill until firm.

Garnish with grapefruit sections and additional whole shrimp, if desired. Serve on lettuce-lined plates.

YIELD: 6 appetizer servings.

BERRY YOGURT GRAPEFRUIT TOPPING

½ *cup diced strawberries*
½ *cup vanilla yogurt*
2 *Florida grapefruit*
4 *whole strawberries*

In small bowl, combine strawberries and yogurt; mix well; chill. Slice grapefruit in half. Remove core. Cut around each section, loosening fruit from membrane. Spoon strawberry-yogurt topping over each grapefruit half.

Garnish with whole strawberry.

YIELD: 4 servings.

Try for breakfast or as a dessert.

7-MINUTE GRAPEFRUIT

2 *Florida grapefruit*
¼ *cup sour cream, divided*
¼ *cup brown sugar, divided*

Cut grapefruit in half. Cut around each section to loosen from membrane. Place halves in 2-quart baking dish. Spread 2 tablespoons sour cream over each half, covering surface. Sprinkle each half with brown sugar. Broil 4 to 6 minutes or until brown sugar is bubbly. Serve warm.

YIELD: 4 servings.

ELEGANT GRAPEFRUIT

While there are many ways to begin a meal, few are quite so elegant and refreshing as a fresh Florida grapefruit half. An imaginatively topped half makes every meal more special. A variety of foods can be used to add color and textural contrast to this zesty fruit.

To prepare grapefruit, cut in half, with a straight cut or with attractive scallop shapes. Remove the core, if desired. Cut around each section, loosening the fruit from the membrane. Serve adorned in one of the following ways:

Salami and Cream Cheese. For each prepared grapefruit half, cut a salami slice in half and roll to form cornucopias. Pipe softened cream cheese into the centers. Arrange on grapefruit and garnish with sprig of parsley.

Granola and Apple. Arrange sliced apples, pinwheel fashion, around each prepared grapefruit half. Sprinkle with your favorite granola-type cereal.

Red Caviar and Sour Cream. Place a dollop of sour cream in the center of each prepared grapefruit half and sprinkle generously with red caviar.

Anchovy, Egg, and Pimiento. Arrange two hard-cooked egg slices on each prepared grapefruit half. Cover with two anchovies and two strips of pimiento.

Cottage Cheese and Kiwi. Arrange peeled kiwi slices on each prepared grapefruit half and cover with a small scoop of cottage cheese.

Yogurt and Toasted Coconut. Place a dollop of yogurt in the center of each prepared grapefruit half. Sprinkle with toasted, shredded coconut. For a sweeter variation, use a fruit yogurt, such as strawberry or cherry.

Photograph, opposite page.

Desserts

Desserts

Desserts made with Florida citrus have a character uniquely their own. They tantalize the senses with sunny colors and tropical fragrances and their taste is one of natural goodness. What is more, the natural sweetness of citrus means less refined sugar in most desserts.

Let dessert be the piéce de résistance, the sweet-satisfying grand finale to a memorable meal. Citrus embellishes a wide variety of old and new favorites. Here is the chef's opportunity to turn culinary artistry into cloud-like meringues and souffles, glorious fruit tarts, creamy custards, frozen delights, cookies, handsome cakes and pies brimming with succulent fruit.

When time is of the essence, choose from several quick and easy recipes scattered throughout this chapter. Of course, fresh citrus fruit, served plain or with cheese and nuts, is also simple, elegant and classically European.

Desserts made with citrus can range from light and energizing to the fantastically rich. The truth is sweet and good: citrus is today's fresh dessert.

Opening photograph, 1-r: Fresh
Florida Ambrosia, page 140; Orange
Dessert Pie, page 137

This dessert and the one that follows, the Orange Custard Tart, are similar recipes. One features sectioned oranges, the other features glazed oranges. Both are beautiful, both taste fabulous.

ORANGE DESSERT PIE

1	9-inch tart shell, baked
⅓	cup all-purpose flour
⅓	cup sugar
1½	cups milk
2	large eggs
½	teaspoon almond extract
8	Florida oranges, peeled and sectioned

Prepare tart shell.*

In medium saucepan, mix flour and sugar. Beat together milk and eggs in a small mixing bowl. Gradually stir milk mixture into flour and sugar in saucepan.

Cook over low heat, stirring constantly, until custard thickens. Remove from heat; add almond extract. Place piece of plastic wrap directly on surface of filling. Cool. Spoon custard into prepared tart shell. Chill.

Before serving, arrange orange sections over custard.

YIELD: 1 9-inch pie.

*TART SHELL

1⅓	cups unsifted all-purpose flour
¼	cup sugar
½	cup butter or margarine, at room temperature
2	egg yolks

Preheat oven to 400°F.

In a medium bowl, mix flour and sugar. Add butter and egg yolks; stir with a fork until mixture clings together in a ball. Press dough into a 9-inch tart pan with removable bottom. Chill 15 minutes.

Bake in a 400°F. oven 10 minutes (no need to prick bottom); reduce oven to 350°F. Bake 10 to 15 minutes longer or until shell is lightly browned. Transfer to wire rack. Cool completely.

YIELD: 1 9-inch baked tart shell.
Photograph, page 135.

ORANGE CUSTARD TART

1	9-inch tart shell, baked
⅓	cup sugar
3	tablespoons cornstarch
1	cup light cream or half-and-half
4	egg yolks, beaten
⅓	cup Florida orange juice
1	teaspoon grated orange peel

Prepare baked tart shell, page 137.

In a small saucepan, mix sugar and cornstarch. Gradually stir in light cream; stir over low heat until very thick. Beat into egg yolks; return mixture to pan and stir in orange juice and peel.

Cook over low heat until thickened, about 5 minutes. Pour into a small bowl. Place a piece of plastic wrap or wax paper directly on the surface of the filling. Chill until very cold.

To assemble tart, spread custard filling evenly in prepared tart shell. Top with Glazed Orange Slices*, ar ranging them in a spoke-like design. Chill. Garnish with mint sprigs, if desired. Orange Custard Tart is best if served within 3 hours after it is assembled.

YIELD: 1 9-inch tart.

*GLAZED ORANGE SLICES

1	Florida orange
⅓	cup orange marmalade
1	tablespoon Florida orange juice

Cut orange in half lengthwise. Place, cut-side-down, on cutting board and cut crosswise into very thin slices. Remove and discard seeds.

In a medium skillet, heat marmalade and orange juice. Add orange slices, a few at a time, and cook 15 to 25 seconds, turning once to glaze each side. Transfer to plate; repeat with remaining slices until all orange slices are glazed. Cover. Chill.

YIELD: 1 to 1½ cups.
Photograph, page 173.

TANGERINE TARTS

Pastry for one 9-inch 2-crust pie
1½   *cups Florida tangerine juice*
1   *cup sugar*
3   *teaspoons grated tangerine peel*
⅔   *cup sweet (unsalted) butter or margarine*
8   *eggs, beaten*
4   *Florida tangerines, peeled and sectioned*

Prepare pastry dough, page 143, doubling recipe.

Preheat oven to 400° F. On a lightly floured surface, roll pastry dough out ⅛-inch thick. Cut out 8 to 10 5-inch circles with a cookie cutter. Press each circle into a 3½-inch fluted tart pan; prick with a fork. Place pans on a cookie sheet. Bake in a 400°F. oven 10 to 12 minutes, or until lightly browned. Cool on a wire rack. Carefully remove shells from pans, cool thoroughly.

In the top of a double boiler over simmering, not boiling water, combine tangerine juice, sugar, peel and butter. Stir until sugar dissolves and butter melts. Gradually whisk about 2 cups of the tangerine mixture into beaten eggs, then return mixture to top of double boiler. Stir constantly until mixture thickens. Cover. Chill.

Before serving, spoon mixture into tart shells. Top each tart with tangerine sections.

YIELD: 8 to 10 tarts.

In Greek and Roman mythology, ambrosia was the food of the gods. Gourmets have long considered ambrosia the perfect light dessert as the finale to a many-course meal. Valencia oranges, ideal for sectioning and slicing, are especially good in this dessert.

FRESH FLORIDA AMBROSIA

2   small Florida grapefruit, peeled and sectioned
3   Florida oranges, peeled and sectioned
1   cup sliced fresh strawberries
½   cup flaked coconut
     Fresh mint leaves (optional)

Combine all ingredients; mix lightly. Chill. Just before serving, garnish with fresh mint, if desired.

YIELD: 4 servings.
Photograph, page 134.

GRAPEFRUIT BREAD PUDDING

15   thin slices French or Italian bread
2½   tablespoons butter or margarine, softened
⅓   cup raisins
2   cups milk
1   cup Florida grapefruit juice
4   eggs, slightly beaten
⅓   cup plus 2 tablespoons firmly packed light brown sugar, divided
½   teaspoon grated grapefruit peel
¼   teaspoon ground cinnamon
2   Florida grapefruit, sectioned

Preheat oven to 350°F.

Spread one side of each bread slice with butter. In a 1½-quart shallow baking dish, arrange bread, buttered-side down and sprinkle with raisins.

In a medium bowl, beat together milk, grapefruit juice, eggs, ⅓ cup brown sugar, grapefruit peel and cinnamon until combined. Pour over bread slices; let stand 30 minutes.

Place baking dish in a pan of hot water. Bake in a 350°F. oven 45 minutes to 1 hour or until tip of a knife inserted in center comes out clean. Remove pan from oven, top with grapefruit slices and remaining 2 tablespoons brown sugar. Broil 2 to 3 minutes or until sugar melts.

YIELD: 6 to 8 servings.
Photograph, opposite page.

Grapefruit Bread Pudding

GRAPEFRUIT-PINEAPPLE PIE

1	*9-inch pastry shell, baked*
1	*cup flaked coconut, toasted, divided*
1	*can (8 ounces) crushed pineapple*
2	*envelopes unflavored gelatine*
2½	*cups Florida grapefruit sections, divided*
1	*can (14 ounces) sweetened condensed milk*
2	*egg whites*
¼	*teaspoon cream of tartar*
½	*cup Florida grapefruit sections (optional)*

Prepare pastry shell*; cool.

To toast coconut, spread in a shallow baking pan. Bake in 350°F. oven for 7 to 12 minutes, stirring frequently until golden brown.

Drain pineapple, measuring liquid. Add enough water, if necessary, to measure ¼ cup. In a small saucepan, combine pineapple liquid and gelatine. Cook over low heat, stirring constantly, until gelatine is dissolved.

Cut 2 cups of grapefruit sections into small pieces. In medium bowl, combine grapefruit pieces, crushed pineapple and condensed milk; mix well. Stir in gelatine mixture. In small bowl of electric mixer, combine egg whites and cream of tartar. Beat until stiff peaks form. Fold egg whites into grapefruit mixture.

Sprinkle ½ cup toasted coconut in bottom of prepared pastry shell. Spoon grapefruit mixture over coconut. Chill until firm. To serve, garnish pie with remaining ½ cup grapefruit sections, if desired, and remaining ½ cup toasted coconut.

YIELD: 1 9-inch pie.

continued

*PASTRY SHELL

    1   cup all-purpose flour
    ¼   teaspoon salt
    ¼   cup butter, at room temperature
    3   tablespoons vegetable shortening
2 to 6   tablespoons ice water

Preheat oven to 475°F.

To make pastry shell, sift flour and salt together into bowl. Using pastry blender, cut in butter and shortening until mixture is the size of small peas. Sprinkle on water, 1 tablespoon at a time, tossing mixture with pastry blender or a fork. When mixture holds together when pinched between thumb and forefinger, stop adding water.

Gather mixture into a ball and turn out onto floured surface. Continue forming into a ball and roll with floured rolling pin to desired size. To place crust in pie plate, fold pastry gently in half and transfer to pie plate, placing folded edge in center of plate. Unfold to cover plate and pat pastry firmly into plate. Avoid stretching the pastry. Trim edges evenly with a scissors or sharp knife, allowing approximately ½-inch edge beyond pie plate.

To finish edge of crust, you may make a rippled fluting by pulling the edge, held by right thumb and forefinger, down and over toward you slightly, holding back the edge with the other hand. Place thumb and finger, held about ½-inch apart, where those of right hand were, and repeat.

Place pie weights on crust to hold it in place while baking. Bake at 475°F. approximately 8 minutes or until golden brown.

YIELD: 1 9-inch pastry shell.

Be imaginative with the Orange Peel Preserves recipe featured here. It is good as a garnish for desserts, meats and fruit relishes.

ORANGE PEEL PRESERVES

4   large Florida oranges
     Water
2   cups granulated sugar

Peel oranges and cut peel into thin slivers. (Use orange segments in another recipe or for eating fresh). Put peel into a 2-quart saucepan and add water to cover. Bring to a boil over high heat and boil 5 minutes. Drain and discard water.

Return peel to pan and add 2 cups water and sugar. Bring to a boil and boil 30 to 45 minutes over moderate heat until very thick and syrupy. Remove from heat and chill until ready to use.

YIELD: 2 cups.

GRAPEFRUIT WITH BERRIES AND CREAM

2   Florida grapefruit
1   cup sour cream, divided
4   teaspoons brown sugar, divided
⅔   cup fresh blueberries
⅔   cup fresh raspberries

To flute grapefruit, pencil a zig-zag guideline around the center of the fruit. Insert a small knife into the core of the fruit at an angle to make one side of a point. Remove the knife; insert to form the opposite side of the point. Do not push the knife in more than halfway. Continue around the fruit, following the line to keep halves equal in size. To separate, gently pull halves apart.

Spoon ¼ cup sour cream on each grapefruit half; sprinkle with 1 teaspoon brown sugar. Spoon berries around cream.

YIELD: 4 servings.
Photograph, back cover.

Its own natural dish makes this multi-colored dessert a delight for both children and adults.

SCALLOPED FRUIT CUP

4   Florida oranges
1   cup strawberries
1   cup honeydew balls
     Fresh mint leaves (optional)

Pencil semicircles around orange, ⅓ of the way down from stem end. Insert a small knife into the core of the fruit and trace along the penciled line. Do not push the knife in more than halfway. To separate, gently pull apart.

With sharp knife, carefully cut fruit from inside shell; section fruit.

Combine orange sections, strawberries and honeydew. Spoon into hollowed orange shells. Garnish with fresh mint, if desired.

YIELD: 4 servings.

Photograph, front cover.

TAMPA GRAPEFRUIT PIE

1   9-inch pastry shell, baked
1   envelope unflavored gelatine
⅓   cup sugar
⅛   teaspoon salt
½   cup cold water
½   cup Florida grapefruit juice
2   cups Florida grapefruit sections, drained, cut in pieces
½   cup heavy cream, whipped

Prepare pastry shell, page 143.

In medium saucepan, combine gelatine, sugar and salt. Stir in water and grapefruit juice. Let stand 1 minute. Stir over low heat until gelatine is completely dissolved, about 5 minutes. Chill until slightly thickened.

Add grapefruit sections to ¾ of the gelatine mixture; spoon into prepared pastry shell. Fold whipped cream into remaining gelatine mixture. Spoon over grapefruit layer. Chill until firm.

YIELD: 1 9-inch pie.

PINK GRAPEFRUIT PARFAIT PIE

1	9-inch pastry shell, baked
1	envelope unflavored gelatine
½	cup Florida pink grapefruit juice
1	pint vanilla ice cream, melted
2	egg whites
2	tablespoons sugar
2	cups Florida pink grapefruit sections, cut in pieces
½	cup heavy cream, whipped (optional)
1	cup Florida pink grapefruit sections (optional)

Prepare pastry shell, page 143.

In a small saucepan, mix gelatine with grapefruit juice. Let stand 1 minute. Stir over low heat until gelatine is completely dissolved. Remove from heat.

Stir in ice cream. Chill, stirring occasionally, until mixture is the consistency of unbeaten egg whites.

In medium bowl, beat egg whites until soft peaks form; gradually add sugar and beat until stiff. Fold into gelatine mixture. Fold in grapefruit sections. Turn into prepared pastry shell. Chill until firm.

Garnish with additional grapefruit sections and whipped cream, if desired.

YIELD: 1 9-inch pie.

Photograph, opposite page.

Pink Grapefruit Parfait Pie

All berries are good combined with grapefruit.

GRAPEFRUIT BLUEBERRY BAKE

2	*cups Florida grapefruit sections*
2	*cups fresh blueberries*
½ to ¾	*cup sugar (depending on sweetness of fruit)*
2	*tablespoons plus 1 cup flour, divided*
½	*teaspoon cinnamon*
4	*tablespoons butter or margarine, divided*
1½	*teaspoons baking powder*
	Pinch salt
⅓	*cup milk*

Preheat oven to 375°F.

In a shallow 1 ½-quart baking dish, combine grapefruit sections and blueberries.

In a small bowl, combine sugar, 2 tablespoons flour and cinnamon; sprinkle over fruit. Dot with 2 tablespoons butter.

In small bowl, sift together remaining 1 cup flour, baking powder and salt. Cut in remaining 2 tablespoons butter until mixture resembles coarse meal. Add milk and stir to make a soft dough.

Pat out on lightly floured board; cut into diamonds. Arrange diamonds over fruit. Bake in a 375°F. oven 25 to 30 minutes or until brown.

Serve with ice cream or whipped cream, if desired.

YIELD: 6 servings.

Minted Grapefruit Ice can also act as an excellent sorbet.

MINTED GRAPEFRUIT ICE

½   cup plus 1 tablespoon sugar, divided
1½   teaspoons unflavored gelatine (½ of envelope)
½   cup water
1   teaspoon dried mint leaves
3   cups Florida grapefruit juice
1   egg white

In a small saucepan, mix ½ cup sugar and gelatine. Add water and mint. Let stand 1 minute. Bring to a boil over moderate heat, stirring constantly, until gelatine dissolves. Remove from heat. Cover. Let stand 10 minutes.

Pour grapefruit juice into a large metal bowl. Strain gelatine mixture through a very fine sieve or several layers of cheese cloth to remove mint leaves. Stir gelatine mixture into grapefruit juice.

Freeze 3 hours or until ice crystals form, 2-inches deep, all around edge of bowl. Mix well with a wire whisk to break up crystals. Freeze 1½ to 2 hours longer or until firm.

Beat egg white until soft peaks form; add remaining 1 tablespoon sugar, beat until stiff peaks form. Beat grapefruit ice with an electric mixer until smooth; fold in beaten egg white. Freeze 1 hour; stir and freeze until firm.

Serve with Frosted Grapes.*

YIELD: 10 to 12 servings.

*FROSTED GRAPES

1   bunch seedless green grapes, cut in small clusters
1   egg white, slightly beaten
3   tablespoons sugar

Brush grapes with egg white and sprinkle with sugar. Set on wire rack and let dry.

Photograph, page 173.

The orange shells of this divine dessert are prepared and chilled ahead of time. Only minutes are needed for assembly before serving.

DANISH ORANGE DELIGHTS

6	*Florida oranges*
¼	*teaspoon rum extract*
1	*cup diced pound cake*
½	*cup chopped semi-sweet chocolate or mini semi-sweet chocolate morsels*
½	*cup chopped pecans*
¼	*cup heavy cream, whipped*

Cut off and discard a 1-inch slice from the top of each of 4 oranges. Using a sharp knife, cut a zig-zag edge around top of oranges. Using a spoon, scoop out pulp; process in a blender or food processor to make juice. Reserve orange juice and shells.

Peel remaining 2 oranges and section; cut sections into ½-inch pieces. In a bowl, mix orange pieces with ⅔ cup of the orange juice and rum extract. Cover, chill 1 to 2 hours.

Just before serving, add cake, chocolate and nuts; spoon into orange shells. Top with whipped cream. Serve immediately.

YIELD: 4 servings.

Photograph, opposite page.

Bavarian Cookie Wreaths, back, page 152; Danish Orange Delights, front

Use various decorations for special holidays—or serve plain!

BAVARIAN COOKIE WREATHS

3½   cups unsifted all-purpose flour
1   cup sugar, divided
3   teaspoons grated orange peel, divided
¼   teaspoon salt
1⅓   cups butter or margarine
¼   cup Florida orange juice
⅓   cup finely chopped blanched almonds
1   egg white beaten with 1 teaspoon water

Preheat oven to 400°F.

In a large bowl, mix flour, ¾ cup sugar, 2 teaspoons orange peel and salt. Using a pastry blender, cut in butter and orange juice until mixture holds together. Knead a few times and press into a ball.

Shape dough into ¾-inch balls; lightly roll each on a floured board into a 6-inch-long strip. Using two strips, twist together to make a rope. Pinch ends of rope together to make a wreath; place on lightly greased baking sheet.

In a shallow dish, mix almonds with remaining ¼ cup sugar and 1 teaspoon orange peel. Brush the top of each wreath with egg white mixture and sprinkle with sugar-almond mixture.

Bake in a 400°F. oven 8 to 10 minutes or until lightly browned. Remove to wire racks; cool completely. Frost if desired.*

YIELD: 5 dozen cookies.

Photograph, page 151.

continued

*FROSTING

1 cup confectioners' sugar
2 tablespoons butter or margarine, at room temperature
1 to 2 teaspoons milk
Few drops green food color
Red cinnamon candies

In a small bowl, mix confectioners' sugar, butter, 1 teaspoon milk and a few drops green food color. Add more milk if necessary to make frosting thick, but spreadable.

Fill a pastry bag fitted with a small leaf tip (preferably #67). Decorate each wreath with 3 or 4 leaves and red-cinnamon-candy berries.

ORANGE-CHOCOLATE SUGAR PLUMS

2 cups coarsely chopped pecans
2 cups coarsely chopped, unblanched almonds
1 cup Orange Peel Preserves, chopped
½ cup flaked coconut
¼ cup Florida orange juice
1 package (8 ounces) semi-sweet chocolate
1 large egg
Confectioners' sugar

In a large bowl, mix pecans, almonds, Orange Peel Preserves,* coconut and orange juice.

In a small saucepan, melt chocolate over moderately low heat; remove from heat and cool 15 minutes. Beat in egg until mixture is well-blended. Stir chocolate into nut mixture. When thoroughly mixed, chill 30 to 45 minutes until firm enough to handle. Shape into walnut-size balls. Roll ½ of the candies in confectioners' sugar. Chill candies until ready to serve.

YIELD: 2½ pounds candy or about 75 pieces.

*Recipe for Orange Peel Preserves, page 144.

Photograph, page 157.

A spotlessly clean and dry mixing bowl and beaters help insure stiff meringues.

ORANGE MARZIPAN MERINGUES

1	can (8 ounces) marzipan or almond paste
4	teaspoons grated orange peel
2	egg whites, at room temperature
⅛	teaspoon cream of tartar
½	cup superfine granulated sugar
	Sugar for sprinkling

Preheat oven to 250°F.

Lightly grease and flour 2 baking sheets; set aside.

Knead marzipan and orange peel until well-blended. Divide in half, roll each half with fingertips into a 15-inch-long strip. Cut strips into ¾-inch pieces; roll each into a ball.

In small bowl of electric mixer, beat egg whites and cream of tartar at high speed until stiff peaks form. Gradually add sugar, about 1 tablespoon at a time, beating until whites are stiff and glossy and all sugar is dissolved. Dip orange marzipan balls into meringue, coating completely; spoon each onto prepared baking sheets, making sure each marzipan ball is completely surrounded in meringue.

Sprinkle each meringue with sugar. Bake in a 250°F. oven 55 to 60 minutes. Transfer to wire racks to cool completely.

YIELD: 3 dozen candies.

A perfect tea or cocktail bread.

ORANGE WALNUT BREAD

2¼   cups unsifted, all-purpose flour
¾   cup sugar
1   tablespoon grated orange peel
2¼   teaspoons baking powder
½   teaspoon salt
¼   teaspoon baking soda
1   cup Orange Peel Preserves*, finely chopped
½   cup mixed candied fruit, finely chopped
2   tablespoons shortening
1   large egg
¾   cup Florida orange juice
1   cup chopped walnuts

Preheat oven to 350°F.

Grease a 9 x 5 x 3-inch loaf pan; set aside. In a large bowl, mix flour, sugar, grated orange peel, baking powder, salt and baking soda. Add Orange Peel Preserves* and candied fruit; toss to coat fruit. Add shortening, egg and orange juice; stir with wooden spoon until dry ingredients are moistened. Stir in nuts.

Spread batter evenly into prepared pan. Bake in a 350°F. oven 50 to 60 minutes or until a cake tester inserted in center of bread comes out clean. Remove from oven, cool 5 minutes. Turn out of pan; cool completely on wire rack. Wrap tightly in plastic wrap or in foil; let stand 24 hours before serving.

YIELD: One 9 x 5 x 3 -inch loaf.

*Recipe for Orange Peel Preserves, page 144.

Photograph, page 157.

SUGAR-DUSTED SNOWFLAKES

½ cup Florida orange juice
⅓ cup milk
1 tablespoon butter or margarine
1 cinnamon stick, 3 inches long
2 cups unsifted all-purpose flour
1½ teaspoons grated orange peel
⅛ teaspoon baking powder
Vegetable oil for frying
Confectioners' sugar

In a small saucepan, combine orange juice, milk, butter and cinnamon stick. (Mixture will curdle). Bring to a boil over high heat; remove from heat, let stand 15 minutes. Remove and discard cinnamon stick.

In a large bowl, mix flour, orange peel and baking powder; make a well in the center. Add warm milk mixture all at once and stir with a wooden spoon, gradually incorporating the flour mixture, until all dry ingredients are moistened.

Turn out onto a very well-floured surface and knead 2 or 3 times until smooth. Cover, let stand 20 minutes. During this time, the dough will cool and become less sticky.

Divide dough in half; roll half on a well-floured surface to ⅛-inch thickness. Using a floured 3-inch star or round cookie cutter, cut dough into shapes. Place on a paper towel and let dry 10 minutes or until top surface is dry to the touch. Repeat with remaining dough, rolling scraps together. Cut out small designs in each cookie with canape cutters, so cookie resembles a snowflake.

Pour enough oil in a medium skillet to depth of 1 inch. Heat to 350°F. on a deep fry thermometer. Fry cookies, 2 or 3 at a time, turning once until very lightly browned. Drain on paper towels. When cool, sprinkle liberally with confectioners' sugar.

YIELD: 3 dozen cookies.

Photograph, opposite page.

Orange Chocolate Sugarplums, top, page 153; Orange Marzipan Meringues, right, page 154; Sugar Dusted Snowflakes, left; Orange Walnut Bread, bottom, page 155

OLD-FASHIONED ORANGE ICE CREAM

2   *cups milk*
4   *eggs, lightly beaten*
1   *cup sugar*
2   *cups (1 pint) heavy cream*
1   *can (12 ounces) Florida frozen concentrated orange juice, thawed, undiluted*

In top of a double boiler, over simmering water, combine milk, eggs and sugar. Cook, stirring constantly, until mixture thickens. Cool. Stir in orange juice concentrate and heavy cream.

Transfer mixture to an ice cream maker. Freeze according to manufacturers' directions. Or, turn into freezer trays or loaf pans and freeze 2 to 3 hours or until almost firm. Turn mixture into bowl; beat until light and fluffy. Pour into freezer trays. Freeze 3 to 4 hours or until completely firm.

YIELD: About 2 quarts.

Sorbet is often served as dessert, as well as before a main course.

TANGERINE SORBET

½   *cup sugar*
1   *envelope unflavored gelatine*
3   *cups Florida tangerine juice, divided*
1   *teaspoon grated tangerine peel*

In a medium bowl, combine sugar and gelatine. Heat 1 cup tangerine juice to boiling. Add to gelatine and stir until gelatine is completely dissolved. Stir in remaining 2 cups juice and grated peel. Cool. Pour into ice cube trays or a 9x9-inch metal pan; cover and freeze.

When almost frozen, scrape into a large mixing bowl. Beat until smooth, but still frozen. Return mixture to pan; cover and freeze until almost frozen. Again scrape into mixing bowl and beat. Spoon into pan, cover and freeze until firm. Serve.

YIELD: About 1 quart.

GRAPEFRUIT SURPRISE

1	cup plus 3 tablespoons sugar, divided
¼	cup cornstarch
½	teaspoon salt
3	eggs, separated
2	cups milk
3	tablespoons butter or margarine
1	teaspoon vanilla
3	large Florida grapefruit

In medium saucepan, combine 1 cup sugar, cornstarch and salt. Gradually add milk and egg yolks; mix well. Cook over low heat, stirring constantly until mixture boils. Boil 1 minute. Remove from heat. Stir in butter and vanilla. Cover surface of pudding with plastic wrap; chill.

Meanwhile, prepare grapefruit. Cut grapefruit in half. Using grapefruit knife, section fruit; drain. Remove all membrane from grapefruit shells. Fill grapefruit shells with sections. Spoon chilled pudding over sections.

In small bowl, beat egg whites until foamy. Gradually beat in remaining 3 tablespoons sugar, beating until stiff peaks form. Spoon or pipe meringue evenly over pudding.

Place grapefruit shells on cookie sheet. Place under broiler about 2 minutes until meringue is golden. Watch carefully to avoid burning. Serve immediately.

YIELD: 6 servings.

You don't have to go through a six-hour routine to surprise your guests and family with truly gala desserts.

SUMMER BREEZE PARFAIT

2	cups Florida grapefruit sections
2	ripe bananas, sliced
½	cup Florida grapefruit juice
¼	teaspoon ground cinnamon
1	cup coconut macaroon crumbs
½	cup heavy cream, whipped
¼	cup toasted, slivered almonds

In medium bowl, combine grapefruit sections, bananas, grapefruit juice and cinnamon; mix well. In parfait glasses or dessert dishes, alternately layer fruit mixture with macaroon crumbs. Top each with whipped cream and almonds. Serve immediately.

YIELD: 4 servings.

COUPE CHARTREUSE

1	Florida grapefruit, peeled and sectioned
2	Florida oranges, peeled and sectioned
2	scoops (½ cup each) raspberry sherbet
⅓	cup Chartreuse liqueur or creme de menthe
	Fresh mint leaves

Arrange citrus sections in 2 dessert dishes. Top with scoop of sherbet. Pour Chartreuse over each serving.

Garnish with mint leaves.

YIELD: 2 servings.

GINGERED SOUFFLE CAKE

2	*envelopes unflavored gelatine*
1	*cup sugar, divided*
¼	*teaspoon salt*
4	*large eggs, separated*
2½	*cups Florida grapefruit juice*
1	*teaspoon chopped candied ginger*
2	*packages (3 ounces each) lady fingers, split*
1	*cup heavy cream, whipped*

In a medium saucepan, mix gelatine, ⅔ cup sugar and salt. In medium bowl, beat together egg yolks and grapefruit juice; stir into gelatine mixture. Cook over low heat, stirring constantly, until gelatine dissolves and mixture thickens slightly, about 5 minutes. Remove from heat; stir in ginger and grapefruit peel.

Chill, stirring occasionally, until mixture mounds slightly when dropped from a spoon.

Beat egg whites until soft peaks form, gradually beat in remaining ⅓ cup sugar; beat until stiff peaks form. Fold egg whites into grapefruit mixture. Fold in whipped cream.

Turn into a 9-inch springform pan lined with lady fingers. Chill 4 to 5 hours, until firm. Remove cake from pan.

Garnish with whipped cream.

YIELD: 8 to 10 servings.

NOTE: To line pan with lady fingers, line sides with rounded side of split lady finger against pan. Then place split lady fingers on bottom of pan very close together so there are no holes.

TANGERINE SOUFFLE WITH APRICOT SAUCE

6	large eggs, separated
1¼	cups sugar, divided
2	envelopes unflavored gelatine
⅛	teaspoon salt
2	tablespoons grated tangerine peel
1½	cups Florida tangerine juice (5 to 6 tangerines)
2	cups heavy cream
3	Florida tangerines, peeled, sectioned, and seeded (gently remove peel, reserve for later use)

Fold a 30-inch piece of wax paper in half lengthwise. Tape securely around a 2-quart souffle dish forming a collar 3 inches above the rim of the dish.

Beat egg yolks lightly. In top of double boiler, mix ¾ cup sugar, gelatine, salt and grated tangerine peel. Stir in beaten egg yolks and tangerine juice. Set top of double boiler over simmering water. Cook, stirring constantly, until mixture is slightly thickened, about 10 minutes. Chill until mixture mounds slightly when dropped from a spoon.

In large mixing bowl, beat egg whites until foamy; gradually beat in remaining ½ cup sugar; beat until stiff, glossy peaks form. Fold into tangerine mixture.

Whip cream until soft peaks form. Fold gently into tangerine mixture. Spoon ⅓ tangerine mixture into souffle dish. Arrange sections from 1 tangerine over souffle. Repeat. Top with souffle mixture. Refrigerate 3 to 4 hours until set.

Garnish with remaining tangerine sections and Candied Tangerine Peel.** Serve with Apricot Sauce*.

YIELD: 10 to 12 servings.

continued

Tangerine Souffle with Apricot Sauce

*APRICOT SAUCE

1 *can (1 pound) apricot halves, drained*
½ *cup Florida tangerine juice (2 to 3 fresh tangerines)*
2 *teaspoons sugar*

In container of electric blender, combine all ingredients. Cover. Process until smooth. Chill. Serve with Tangerine Souffle.

YIELD: 2 cups.

**CANDIED TANGERINE PEEL

 Reserved peel from 3 Florida tangerines
¼ *cup water*
1 *cup sugar, divided*

With sharp knife gently scrape white membrane from peel. Cut peel lengthwise into thin strips. In small saucepan, bring water and ½ cup sugar to boiling; stir until sugar is dissolved. Add peel, simmer over medium heat 5 minutes, stirring frequently. Turn peel into a strainer, drain thoroughly. Cool on wax paper. Roll peel in ½ cup sugar.

Serve with Tangerine Souffle.

YIELD: About ¾ cup.

Photograph, page 163.

An Old English favorite.

FROSTED GRAPEFRUIT TRIFLE

1	package pound cake (about 10 ounces) cut in 14 slices
1	cup flaked coconut, divided
1	can (8¼ ounces) crushed pineapple, drained
½	cup canned cream of coconut
1	Florida grapefruit, peeled and sectioned
1¾	cups Florida grapefruit juice
1	cup heavy cream, whipped

In a 1½-quart bowl or casserole, arrange enough cake slices to cover bottom and sides of bowl; sprinkle with ⅓ cup coconut. In small bowl, combine pineapple and cream of coconut; pour half the mixture over cake. Layer all the grapefruit sections over pineapple. Repeat with remaining cake, coconut and pineapple, ending with coconut. Pour grapefruit juice over all.

Cover; refrigerate 24 hours. Turn upside down onto serving plate. Frost with whipped cream.

YIELD: 6 to 8 servings.

ORANGES PIQUANT

5	Florida oranges, peeled and sectioned
1	cup orange marmalade
½	cup sour cream

Divide orange sections evenly in 8 dessert dishes. Chill thoroughly.

Just before serving, melt marmalade in small saucepan. Spoon over oranges. Top with a dollop of sour cream. Serve immediately.

YIELD: 8 servings.

NOTE: Homemade orange marmalade may be used, if desired, page 129.

Simple foods, simply cooked, with the freshness of the ingredients heightened by preparation, are served with elegance and panache. Poached Oranges perfectly exemplifies the beauty of this type of cooking.

POACHED ORANGES A LA GLORIOUS FOOD

6	medium Florida oranges
	Zest from oranges
2	cups water
1	cup sugar
1	cup Grand Marnier

Peel the zest from two oranges with a vegetable peeler and then cut into very thin julienne strips. Reserve for Orange Zest Grenadine**. Remove pith from oranges and discard. Completely peel remaining 4 oranges.

Bring water and sugar to a boil; cook 8 minutes to form a syrup. Add Grand Marnier.

Place oranges in syrup mixture and poach 10 minutes basting often. Remove from heat, let oranges cool in poaching liquid. Reserve poaching liquid for Grand Marnier Sauce*.

YIELD: 6 servings.

*GRAND MARNIER SAUCE

1	cup reserved poaching liquid
2	cups Florida orange juice
1	teaspoon grated orange peel
1½	tablespoons cornstarch
½	cup creme fraiche

Combine poaching liquid, orange juice and grated orange peel in a small saucepan; cook over medium heat until reduced by half. Mix cornstarch with ¼ cup water; rapidly whisk into boiling mixture. Cook 3 minutes, remove from heat. Cool. Stir in creme fraiche. Keep refrigerated.

Spoon Grand Marnier Sauce onto plate. Place poached orange on top of sauce and sprinkle with Orange Zest Grenadine.**

continued

166

Poached Oranges a la Glorious Food

**ORANGE ZEST GRENADINE

¼   cup grenadine syrup
¼   cup cold water
¼   cup granulated sugar
      Reserved julienne peel from 2 Florida oranges

In a heavy saucepan, combine grenadine, water and sugar. Bring to a boil over high heat and cook 4 minutes. Fold in orange peel julienne and cook 8 minutes longer, stirring constantly. Cool, store in an airtight container in refrigerator until ready to use.

NOTE: This dessert should be served with knife and fork.

Photograph, page 167.

When in season, substitute or include tangerines and tangelos.

CHOCOLATE COVERED CITRUS SECTIONS

4   Florida oranges
2   Florida grapefruit
1   package (12 ounces) chocolate morsels
2   tablespoons vegetable shortening

Line a large tray with wax paper or aluminum foil.

Peel oranges and grapefruit. Remove all pith. Pull apart segments, being careful not to tear membranes.

In top of double boiler over hot, not boiling, water, melt morsels and shortening; stir until smooth. (If mixture seems too thick, add more shortening 1 teaspoon at a time.) Be careful not to let any water drip into chocolate mixture. Remove from heat. Hold fruit on one end and dip to cover ⅔ of each segment. Let excess chocolate drip back into pan. Place dipped segments on waxed paper-lined tray. Refrigerate until ready to serve.

YIELD: About 4 cups fruit.

GINGERED GRAPEFRUIT COMPOTE

¼   *cup slivered grapefruit peel*
4   *cups Florida grapefruit sections (4 medium grapefruit)*
1   *cup water*
¼   *cup sugar*
1   *tablespoon chopped candied ginger*

Remove peel from grapefruit in thin strips, using vegetable peeler. Cut into thin slivers with scissors or knife; measure ¼ cup and reserve.

To section grapefruit, cut slice from top, then cut off peel in strips from top to bottom, cutting deep enough to remove white membrane; then cut slice from bottom. Or cut off peel round and round, spiral fashion. Go over fruit again, removing any remaining white membrane. Cut along side of each dividing membrane from outside to middle of core. Remove section by section over bowl to retain juice from fruit. Drain ½ cup juice from grapefruit sections.

In medium saucepan, mix juice, water, sugar, slivered peel and ginger. Stir over low heat until sugar dissolves. Bring to a boil, reduce heat and simmer 20 minutes, until syrupy. Pour over grapefruit sections. Chill. Serve in stemmed sherbet dishes.

YIELD: 6 servings.

ORANGES VALENTINO

8	*Florida oranges*
2	*cups water, divided*
1	*cup light corn syrup*
¾	*cup sugar*
1	*can (8¼ ounces) crushed pineapple, well drained*
3	*tablespoons slivered candied ginger*
¼	*cup grenadine*

Peel 2 oranges with a vegetable peeler, removing peel in long strips. Cut strips into pieces ⅛-inch wide and 1½-inches long. Peel remaining oranges; discard peel. Place all oranges in large bowl; set aside.

In small saucepan, combine orange strips with 1 cup water. Cover. Bring to boiling. Drain, rinse with cold water.

In medium saucepan, combine remaining 1 cup water, corn syrup and sugar; bring to boiling, stir until sugar dissolves. Cook, uncovered, over medium heat, 10 minutes. Add orange peel, pineapple and ginger. Cover. Cook 30 minutes longer; remove from heat, stir in grenadine.

Pour hot syrup over oranges in serving bowl; cool; cover. Refrigerate 6 hours.

To serve, place whole orange on serving plate, spoon sauce over orange.

YIELD: 8 servings.

NOTE: This dessert should be served with a dessert fork and knife. For easier eating, oranges may be cut in thick slices or wedges before serving.

An unusual and very attractive combination. Substitute tangelos when in season for added variety.

GRAPEFRUIT RHUBARB COBBLER

3	*tablespoons cornstarch*
¼	*cup water*
¾	*cup plus 1 tablespoon sugar, divided*
¾	*cup light corn syrup*
1	*tablespoon butter or margarine*
¼	*teaspoon ground mace*
4	*cups Florida grapefruit sections well-drained*
1	*cup diced, fresh rhubarb*
1¼	*cups packaged biscuit mix*
½	*cup milk*

Preheat oven to 425°F.

In small saucepan, combine cornstarch and water. Stir in ¾ cup sugar and corn syrup. Cook, stirring constantly, over medium heat until mixture boils. Boil 1 minute. Stir in butter and mace. Combine grapefruit and rhubarb in buttered shallow 1½-quart baking dish, pour cornstarch mixture over fruit.

In small bowl, combine biscuit mix, remaining 1 tablespoon sugar and milk; drop by spoonfuls onto grapefruit mixture. Bake in a 425°F. oven 20 to 25 minutes or until biscuit topping is golden brown.

YIELD: 4 to 6 servings.

ORANGE SUNSHINE CAKE

3	*cups unsifted all-purpose flour*
3	*teaspoons baking powder*
½	*teaspoon salt*
1	*cup plus 2 tablespoons unsalted butter or margarine, at room temperature, divided*
2⅓	*cups sugar, divided*
5	*large eggs*
1	*cup Florida orange juice, divided*
2	*teaspoons grated orange peel*

Preheat oven to 350°F.

Grease three 9-inch round cake pans and line bottoms with wax paper cut to fit bottom of pan. In a medium bowl, mix flour, baking powder and salt. In the large bowl of an electric mixer, beat 1 cup butter and 2 cups sugar at medium speed until creamy. Add eggs, one at a time, beating well after each addition.

Beat in flour mixture alternately with ¾ cup orange juice, beating well after each addition. Beat in orange peel. Pour batter evenly into prepared pans. Bake in a 350°F. oven 25 to 30 minutes or until cake tester inserted in center of cakes comes out clean. Remove pans from oven and loosen cakes around edges with a small metal spatula. Turn cakes out onto wire racks; peel off and discard wax paper.

Turn cakes, right-side-up, and prick all over with a wooden pick.

In a small saucepan, melt remaining 2 tablespoons butter, ⅓ cup sugar and ¼ cup orange juice. Cook, stirring until sugar dissolves. Spoon slowly over warm cakes, letting syrup soak in. Let cakes cool completely.

Complete cake with Orange Sunshine Cake Filling* and frost**.

YIELD: 10 to 12 servings.

continued

Minted Grapefruit Ice, top, page 149;
Orange Sunshine Cake, middle;
Orange Custard Tart, bottom, page
138

*ORANGE SUNSHINE CAKE FILLING

⅓   cup plus 2 tablespoons sugar, divided
1½   teaspoons unflavored gelatine
¼   cup Florida orange juice
½   cup unsalted butter or margarine
2   large eggs, separated

In a small saucepan, mix ⅓ cup sugar and gelatine. Add orange juice. Stir over low heat until gelatine dissolves. Add butter, stir until butter melts.

In a small bowl, beat egg yolks; stir in orange mixture; then return mixture to saucepan. Cook over low heat 3 to 5 minutes, stirring until thickened. Cool to room temperature.

Beat egg whites with remaining 2 tablespoons sugar until stiff; fold into cooled orange mixture. Refrigerate until very thick but still spreadable, about 10 minutes. Do not chill too long or mixture will set. Use to fill Orange Sunshine Cake.

YIELD: About 2 cups.

**FROSTING

2	egg whites	2	tablespoons water
⅔	cup sugar	¼	teaspoon cream of tartar
3½	tablespoons light corn syrup	½	teaspoon vanilla extract Slivered orange peel (optional)

In the top of a double boiler, mix egg whites, sugar, corn syrup, water and cream of tartar. Beat with an electric mixer or rotary beater over boiling water 7 minutes or until very stiff and glossy. Remove from heat; beat in vanilla. Use to frost Orange Sunshine Cake.

NOTE: To assemble cake: Place one cake layer on cake plate, spread with half the Orange Filling. Top with second cake layer, spread with Frosting. Top with remaining cake layer and spread with remaining Orange Filling. Frost sides of cake with remaining Frosting. Garnish with slivered orange peel, if desired.

Photograph, page 173.

Also a good and light luncheon salad served on a bed of lettuce with a creamy mayonnaise dressing. Whether served as a dessert or salad, it is ideal for preparing in advance.

FROZEN FRUIT LOAF

4   large eggs, separated
1   cup sugar, divided
¼   cup Florida grapefruit juice
2   cups heavy cream, whipped
1   package (10 ounces) frozen raspberries, thawed
4   Florida grapefruit, sectioned and cut into pieces
   Additional Florida grapefruit sections (optional)
   Mint leaves (optional)

Beat egg yolks in top of double boiler; add ¾ cup sugar and grapefruit juice. Stir over boiling water until thickened, about 3 minutes. Cool to room temperature. In a medium mixing bowl, beat egg whites until foamy. Gradually beat in remaining ¼ cup sugar until stiff peaks form. Fold beaten egg whites into cooled grapefruit mixture. Fold in whipped cream.

Purée raspberries in a blender or food processor. Fold puréed raspberries into ⅓ of the grapefruit mixture. Refrigerate. Add grapefruit pieces to remaining mixture. Pour half the grapefruit mixture with grapefruit sections into a 9 x 5 x 3-inch loaf pan. Freeze until firm, about 1 hour.

Spoon raspberry mixture over frozen layer. Freeze 1 hour until firm. Add remaining grapefruit mixture; freeze until set. Remove from freezer and let stand 5 minutes. Unmold.

Garnish with additional grapefruit sections and mint leaves, if desired.

YIELD: 10 to 12 servings.

ORANGE-PUMPKIN CAKE

2½   *cups sugar*
1   *cup vegetable oil*
4   *large eggs*
1   *can (16 ounces) pumpkin (about 2 cups)*
1   *tablespoon grated orange peel*
3   *cups all-purpose flour*
2   *teaspoons baking soda*
1   *teaspoon cinnamon*
½   *teaspoon salt*
½   *teaspoon baking powder*
½   *teaspoon ground allspice*
⅛   *teaspoon ground clove*
⅔   *cup Florida orange juice*
       Julienne of orange zest

Preheat oven to 350°F.

In large mixing bowl, beat sugar, oil and eggs. Stir in pumpkin and orange peel.

Sift together flour, baking soda, cinnamon, salt, baking powder, allspice and clove. Add to creamed mixture alternately with orange juice.

Pour batter into buttered (12 cup) bundt cake pan. Bake in a 350°F. oven 50 to 55 minutes or until cake tester inserted in center of cake comes out clean. Cool 5 minutes; invert onto wire rack. Cool thoroughly.

Spoon Orange Glaze* over cake.

Garnish with orange zest.

YIELD: 12 to 15 servings.

continued

*ORANGE GLAZE

1½   cups sifted confectioners' sugar
1   teaspoon grated orange peel
1 to 2   tablespoons Florida orange juice

In a small bowl, blend all ingredients to a spreading consistency. Spoon on Orange-Pumpkin Cake.

YIELD: 1½ cups.

Photograph, page 119.

Easy and quick.

SLICED ORANGES DUBLIN

6   tablespoons brown sugar
6   tablespoons butter or margarine
½   cup heavy cream
6   Florida oranges, peeled, sliced

In small saucepan, combine sugar, butter and cream. Stir over low heat until sugar is dissolved and mixture comes to a boil. Simmer 2 minutes.

Arrange orange slices in large bowl or individual dessert dishes. Spoon hot caramel mixture over oranges.

YIELD: 6 servings.

The magical mousse is a French invention from the Middle Ages. By the 14th century, it had become one of the most popular dishes in Great Britain. To this day, the mousse has retained its reputation in Europe as the most elegant finish to a dinner.

ORANGE MOUSSE ORLANDO

1	envelope unflavored gelatine
¼	cup sugar
4	large eggs, separated
½	cup cold water
1	can (6 ounces) Florida frozen concentrated orange juice, thawed, undiluted
⅓	cup hazelnut liqueur (or orange-flavored liqueur)
¼	teaspoon cream of tartar
1	cup heavy cream, whipped
4	Florida oranges, peeled and sectioned
¼	cup toasted slivered almonds or chopped hazelnuts (optional)
1	Florida orange, peeled and sectioned (optional)

In a medium saucepan, combine gelatine and sugar. Beat together egg yolks and water; stir into gelatine mixture. Cook over low heat, stirring constantly, until gelatine dissolves and mixture thickens slightly. Remove from heat; stir in orange juice concentrate and liqueur. Chill, stirring occasionally, until mixture thickens slightly.

Beat egg whites with cream of tartar until stiff; fold into gelatine mixture. Fold in whipped cream.

Arrange orange sections in 8 large balloon wine glasses. Spoon mousse over orange sections. Top with nuts and orange sections, if desired.

YIELD: 8 servings.

SOUSED ORANGE SLICES

This same recipe, using sectioned oranges, makes a wonderful topping for your favorite vanilla ice cream.

2	cups water
1	cup sugar
1	cinnamon stick, 2 inches long
4	whole allspice
⅔	cup orange-flavored liqueur
6	Florida oranges, peeled, sliced

In medium saucepan, combine water and sugar; heat, stirring until sugar is dissolved. Add cinnamon stick and allspice. Boil, uncovered, until mixture is reduced to 1 cup. Cool slightly. Add liqueur; mix well. Transfer mixture to a bowl. Add orange slices. Cover. Refrigerate 5 hours or overnight.

YIELD: 6 to 8 servings.

Photograph, page 79.

ORANGE ZABAGLIONE

A double boiler is necessary here. Do not cook over direct heat. Since this recipe increases in volume as you beat, be sure to choose a large enough pot.

5	egg yolks
1	whole egg
5	tablespoons sugar
½	cup Florida orange juice
1	tablespoon sherry
4	Florida oranges, peeled and sliced
	Cinnamon (optional)

In the top of a large double boiler, beat together until light all ingredients except sliced oranges. Over barely simmering water, beat constantly with portable electric mixer or rotary beater until the mixture foams up, deflates slightly, and becomes thick. This will take about 10 minutes. Serve immediately over sliced oranges.

To serve cold, place the top of the double boiler in a large bowl of ice water after mixture is cooked and thick and beat Zabaglione for 5 minutes, or until cool. Serve or refrigerate several hours, until needed. Serve over sliced oranges, dusted with cinnamon, if desired.

YIELD: 6 servings.

Garnishes

Garnishes

When made with Florida citrus, garnishes are so luscious and eye-catching, they add glamour to the entire meal.

Most importantly, garnishes are fun and easy! A few special knives (such as a zester and channel knife, available commercially), coupled with an imagination and spirit of adventure, are all one needs to turn wallflower garnishes into masterpieces envied by the most honored chefs. As you zest, channel, flute and scallop, you will discover an infinite variety of garnishes using citrus fruit sections and peel.

Also known as rind or zest, the peel is rich in citrus oils, which impart a concentrated yet totally refreshing flavor to every dish, even robust sauces and meats, stews and gravies. Because of its thinner peel, Florida citrus peel curls and shapes so easily, you will be amazed at your own creativity.

Today's garnish not only enhances food flavor and adds color, but it also complements the texture of other foods, creating a new dimension in the entire presentation of the recipe. The garnish has become an integral part of the meal. And what better final touch for any recipe than the fresh and invigorating citrus.

PEELING
Chill Florida oranges and grapefruit before peeling. Slice off both ends of the fruit. Remove peel by cutting strips from the top of the fruit to the bottom. Peel can also be removed by using round strokes in spiral fashion. Cut deep enough to remove white membrane or pith.

SECTIONING
Use chilled, peeled fruit. Cut along the side of each dividing membrane to the core. Remove sections over a container to catch juice.

GRAPEFRUIT HALVES
Cut fruit in half between stem and flower ends. Remove seeds, if any. Insert sharply pointed paring knife in the center at the core, close to the membrane. Cut along membrane from the center to the rind, along the rind and the other membrane back to the center. Repeat for all segments. Be careful not to cut the membrane. To keep fruit steady slice off bottom.

FLUTING
Pencil a zig-zag guideline around the center of the fruit. Insert a small knife into the core of the fruit at an angle to make one side of a point. Remove the knife; insert to form the opposite side of the point. Do not push the knife in more than halfway. Continue around the fruit following the line to keep halves equal in size. To separate, gently pull halves apart.

SCALLOPING
Follow the same steps for fluting, except cut semicircles rather than straight angles.

CHANNELING
Channeling produces a small, even groove running from top to bottom or across an orange or grapefruit. Using a channel knife, a tool with a grooved edge, pull along the peel of the fruit. Channels made at close intervals will produce a channeled edge when a slice is cut vertical to the channeling.

ZESTING
Using long strokes, draw the zester down firmly from top to bottom or across the fruit. Each stroke will produce a very thin strip of peel.

WOVEN CITRUS BASKETS
A basket woven with orange or grapefruit peel can be made by using a wooden base with wicker guides stuck in the base. Use long pieces of orange peel channeled from the fruit to weave in and out of the wicker guides.

CITRUS BASKETS
Make a pencil guideline around the center of an orange or grapefruit. Then mark a ½-inch wide strip across top for basket handle. Cut out sections between marks; remove. With a sharp knife, make a fluted edge around the rim of the basket. Carefully remove citrus from handle and scoop out citrus from basket portion.

CITRUS ROSES
With a sharp paring knife or vegetable peeler start at the top of the fruit and cut in a spiral motion from top to bottom. Remove a continuous, thin, one-inch piece of rind. Do not cut so deeply as to remove pith. For the center of the rose, roll the long piece of peel tightly. Continue wrapping until the rose is formed and all the peel is used. Pinch tightly or secure with a toothpick.

About Citrus

NUTRITION

A wealth of nutrition is sealed into every orange, grapefruit, tangerine and tangelo. One cup of Florida orange or grapefruit juice, or its equivalent fresh fruit, provides more than the National Research Council's recommended daily allowance of Vitamin C.

- Citrus fruits and their juices are very rich sources of Vitamin C, a wondrous and necessary element that performs a myriad of functions, from helping heal cuts and bruises to strengthening teeth and gums to making skin and hair shine with good health.

- Citrus is also an excellent source of potassium and a good source of folic acid, thiamine, Vitamin B6, phosphorus, magnesium, pantothenic acid, riboflavin, niacin and Vitamin A. Fresh citrus contains pectin, which adds needed fiber to our diet, and is especially adept at lowering blood serum cholesterol levels.

- Fresh citrus fruit or fruit juices have negligible quantities of sodium and can be used generously in sodium-restricted diets.

- In addition to its nutritional values, citrus has been a rallying point for generations of weight-watchers. Half of a medium-sized grapefruit has 40 calories and an 8-ounce glass of its juice has only 100 calories.

- Vitamin C is not stored in the body like other vitamins. It must be replenished daily. Make Florida citrus juices and citrus fruit a regular part of your daily eating. Your body will thank you!

The breakfast table is one of the best places at which to maintain a healthy level of Vitamin C. By breakfast time, the body's "fires," usually without solid food for at least 12 hours, are burning low. The body craves a restorative burst of energy to get the day going in a positive and healthy manner. Far too many people skimp on or skip altogether this vital meal.

A well-balanced breakfast should provide one-third to one-fourth of an entire day's nutritional needs! To make the most of this bonanza, start off with a large glass of 100% pure citrus juice.

A recommended menu to accompany citrus juice includes bread, cereal or other whole-grain product and a dairy food. For a heartier meal, add eggs, meat or even peanut butter! No matter what the time of day, when that inner-signal says it is time for an energy boost, make it citrus.

COSMETIC

Florida citrus fruits benefit the body from without as well as from within. Orange and grapefruit peels and juices are natural cosmetics that will keep skin fresh and glowing in a variety of ways.

• For a great natural facial, boil the peels of an orange and grapefruit with 2 cups of non-carbonated mineral water. Strain the liquid into a bottle and apply to face twice daily. Keep refrigerated.

• For a refreshing skin bracer, blend the juice of half a grapefruit with warm water. Splash it on a just washed face to tighten pores.

• For rough, red elbows, dip and rub elbows into grapefruit halves. This will soften elbows in only a few days.

• For softer cuticles and whiter nails, mix 3 cups of warm water with the juice of half a grapefruit. Soak fingers for 5 minutes. Repeat weekly.

Florida citrus has endless cosmetic uses. Test your imagination and create your own citrus beauty secrets.

RIPENESS AND COLOR

Citrus is one of the few fruits on the market that does not continue to ripen after it has been picked. All citrus for sale is fully matured and ready to be eaten.

Florida citrus derives its orange and yellow coloring from a combination of warm days and cool nights. However, a natural phenomenon called "regreening" sometimes makes citrus appear unripe. This occurs when trees send an overdose of chlorophyll into the ripened fruit or if nature's thermometer goes off course and nights remain balmy, often causing the ripening fruit to retain its outer green shading. Fortunately for citrus lovers, the fruit continues developing inside, where it counts, and taste and texture are not affected.

Occasionally, citrus fruit has small brown spots or scratches known as "wind scars," caused by the fruit brushing against tree limbs during heavy winds. Safe inside the peeling, the fruit remains unscathed.

Florida citrus is inspected and packed according to strict Florida standards of maturity. So don't judge a Florida citrus fruit by its color. It's all ripe and all good!

SELECTING

Selecting fresh Florida citrus is a simple job.

- Look for fruit that is heavy for its size. The heavier the fruit, the juicier it will be.

- Also look for citrus fruit that is firm to the touch and free of soft spots.

- Selection of fresh Florida citrus should not be influenced by color. Color has no bearing on ripeness.

Which citrus juices are packed under strict Florida standards? To be sure the orange juice and grapefruit juice you buy is 100% pure and meets Florida's highest standards of excellence, look for the following on the label of your favorite brands.

- On grapefruit juice, look for Florida's Sunshine Tree or the words "100% pure Florida."

- On orange juice containers, look for Florida's Sunshine Tree or the new "Florida's Seal of Approval."

STORING

- Fruit must be properly stored to preserve its flavor and appearance. It is most comfortable, and remains freshest longest, when refrigerated.

- Left in the refrigerator too long, citrus peel can develop dark, sunken patches. After all, it is a sensitive tropical fruit from areas without cold weather. However, natural blemishes on the peel do not affect the fruit's taste.

- If refrigerator space is a problem, fruit can be stored in any cool, dry area.

- Citrus fruit can be maintained at optimum quality for 6 to 8 weeks.

- When storing Florida citrus, do not smother it in plastic bags or wrapping. Drops of moisture can form between the wrapping, causing the fruit to mold.

- Citrus juice is best stored at temperatures of 35 to 40 degrees. Keep juice tightly covered to retain its full nutritional value. For the very best taste, shake or stir juice vigorously before serving.

SEASONS AND TYPES

Research continues to develop new cultivars producing juicier varieties of oranges, grapefruit, tangerines and tangelos.

In winter months, look for Navel, Pineapple, Temple and Parson Brown oranges as well as Dancy tangerines and Orlando tangelos. The Minneola tangelo is available in January. Honey tangerines are in plentiful supply during late winter and spring months and Valencia oranges are available beginning in the spring through July. Hamlin oranges are harvested in the fall.

Grapefruit—Ruby Red, Pink, Marsh Seedless and Duncan—are available throughout the year with the exception of August and September. In these two months, try a variety of recipes using citrus juices.

Index